D1196640

Romance Redux

Romance Redux

Finding Love in Your Later Years

Laura Stassi

HOST OF THE PUBLIC RADIO PODCAST
DATING WHILE GRAY

ROWMAN & LITTLEFIELD
Lanham • Boulder • New York • London

Published by Rowman & Littlefield
An imprint of The Rowman & Littlefield Publishing Group, Inc.
4501 Forbes Boulevard, Suite 200, Lanham, Maryland 20706
www.rowman.com

86-90 Paul Street, London EC2A 4NE

British Library Cataloguing in Publication Information Available

Library of Congress Cataloging-in-Publication Data

Names: Stassi, Laura, author.
Title: Romance redux : finding love in your later years / Laura Stassi.
Description: Lanham, Maryland : Rowman & Littlefield, 2022. | Includes
    bibliographical references and index. | Summary: "Offers insight,
    encouragement, and hope to older adults getting back on the dating scene
    · Includes the author's own experiences as well as those of other gray love
    seekers and finders · Features sidebars that list insider tips gleaned from
    experts the author interviewed · Covers both same-sex and opposite-sex
    relationships"—Provided by publisher.
Identifiers: LCCN 2022002686 | ISBN 9781538168851 (cloth) | ISBN
    9781538168868 (ebook)
Subjects: LCSH: Dating (Social customs) | Older people—Social conditions.
    Host of the public radio podcast 'Dating While Gray.Host of the public radio
    podcast 'Dating While Gray. Love—Social aspects.
Classification: LCC HQ801 .S79 2022 | DDC 306.73—dc23/eng/20220228
LC record available at https://lccn.loc.gov/2022002686

To borrow from the song "Lonely People," written by husband-and-wife songwriting team Dan and Catherine Peek:

This is for all the single people
Thinking that life has left them dry.
Don't give up . . .

~

Contents

~

Introduction

I was married for almost thirty years, and then I got divorced. For the first time in my life, I was on my own. But I wasn't alone. Literally, there are millions of Americans fifty and older who are single. Some of us are solo by choice or because we never found a special someone. Not yet, anyway. Or maybe we were married but then lost our partners to death or divorce. In fact, the divorce rate among older people in long-lasting marriages has exploded since the 1990s. It's a phenomenon occurring worldwide, including in South Africa, Japan, Australia, and England. In some countries, divorce among people fifty and older has been labeled *silver splitting*. In the United States, researchers coined the term *gray divorce*.

A gray divorce—that's what happened to me, unexpectedly. I learned how to feel happy and whole on my own, but I didn't think I wanted to be uncoupled forever. I decided I should at least try to find another romantic partner, but how? I was clueless. The last time I'd been single, I was a teenager. Home telephone answering machines weren't even a thing.

As a writer of articles on health, wellness, and medical issues for military families and author of almost two dozen nonfiction children's books, I'd tackled some big research projects in my career. So I decided to use my professional skills for my personal life. I started digging. I sought advice and information from older people who had found new love for life's later years. I also gathered valuable tips and insights from sociologists, researchers, health and relationship experts, and dating coaches.

I discovered myriad ways to meet potential romantic partners. Hint: Online dating might have seemed the most obvious, but it wasn't the *only* way. I also learned how people addressed some of the unique challenges of partnering in the second half of life. I wanted to share everything I learned, so I launched a website to post true stories I wrote. I called it *Dating While Gray*, because what came after gray divorce? Gray dating! But the website also was for older people who'd been widowed or had short-term marriages or who'd never been married. I used the word *gray* to refer to anyone fifty or older. (It's so much better than *senior* or *elder* or—groan—*geriatric*, right?)

I'd written and posted maybe a half dozen of these stories when, in the summer of 2018, I heard a promotion on WAMU. The NPR member station in Washington, D.C., was launching an incubator called the Pod Shop to find creative projects that could be developed into podcasts. If you're not familiar with the term—and I certainly wasn't, back then—a *podcast* is like a radio show, with a series of episodes built around a theme. However, a podcast is produced as a digital audio file instead of being broadcast over the airwaves. So instead of turning on the radio, listeners access podcasts by downloading the files onto their computer or mobile device. Episodes might be released daily, weekly, or on some other schedule.

Thinking a podcast would be a great way to combine my writing skills with a long-dormant interest in performing, I applied to the Pod Shop. I was one of five people—and the oldest! —selected out of well over five hundred applicants. My fellow Pod Shoppers and I each received a $2,500 stipend to purchase start-up equipment: microphones, a tape recorder, earphones, a subscription to audio-editing software. Then we spent three months learning how to use it all and developing pilot episodes of our respective creative projects. After my long career as a writer, learning how to craft audio stories was the creative rush of a lifetime. Who says you can't teach an older person new tricks?

When the Pod Shop ended, we each had the equipment and knowledge necessary to continue podcasting on our own, if we desired. I was the lucky participant chosen to go to contract with WAMU for a first season of ten episodes. *Dating While Gray* premiered in February 2020; a month later, the COVID-19 pandemic caused the shutdown of every-day life as we all knew it. When WAMU closed its doors, I fashioned a recording studio out of a closet in my spare bedroom and continued working from there, communicating with my producers through Zoom. Thankfully, most of the interviews had already been completed in the station's studios.

As *Dating While Gray* episodes were released on Apple Podcasts, Spotify, Stitcher, and other outlets, I received phone messages, emails, and reviews from listeners all over the world. *Dating While Gray* had a fair share of younger fans, but most were older people. They had com-ments and questions; they also shared their own struggles and successes with seeking, finding, and keeping romantic love. *Dating While Gray* began to feel as much like a social mission as an editorial project. Here are excerpts from communications I received:

⟡

I applaud you for taking this on. . . . No one's talking about these issues.

⟡

I find your program inspirational. Makes me feel that if others can make the change and are at least seeking a rewarding relationship, maybe I can too.

⟡

I have so enjoyed all the episodes. The stories have definitely given me hope and encouragement.

⟡

I'm 51 and at a crossroads in my own marriage. From your podcast, I understand that your divorce was not initially your choice. . . . If you have any advice for me, I'd very much appreciate it.

⟡

Emails continued to crowd my in-box well after season 1 concluded, in May 2020. I turned my attention to a full-time writing job while plotting my next steps. Though *Dating While Gray* had been a success, WAMU decided to discontinue its national podcast unit, and we parted ways. Like many other business organizations, the station was in financial straits because of the pandemic. Adding to the turmoil were serious internal issues related to sexual harassment, diversity, and inclusion.

Thankfully, I soon found a new production and distribution partner: WUNC, North Carolina Public Radio. I left my full-time job in October 2020 to devote all my creative efforts to the podcast. Season 2 episodes were released between mid-February and early May 2021. More favorable listener emails followed, including these:

I love the show and am so glad it's back on! I'm still separated but contemplating dipping my toe in the dating pool.

I started dating about six months ago and wish I had listened to the podcast before I ventured into those waters. I appreciate your work. You are so thoughtful and caring in your interviews.

I wanted to take a moment to offer my thanks for helping me through this rather difficult time in my life. You have answered so many questions, even questions I've not yet thought of. Your insight and research about body changes, grief, gray dating (eventually) is priceless.

When *Dating While Gray* went on hiatus in 2021, I turned my attention back to the writing that sparked the podcast. The result is this book. On the following pages, I share my gray-dating journey as well as the true stories of other gray love seekers, finders, and keepers. I also revisit some of the podcast interviews while including further insights and advice gleaned from dating and relationship experts. Whether you're seeking an opposite-sex or a same-sex partner—or maybe gender identity doesn't matter at all—I hope you'll find inspiration and encouragement. Finding a special someone at this stage of life can feel daunting, even overwhelming. Partnership, though, feels especially relevant in this age of coronavirus. The pandemic forced us all to reconsider how to make and maintain romantic connections and why it may be important to do so.

All of the stories you'll read are true, though some names and identifying details of the nonexpert sources have been changed. It's mostly to ensure we don't mortify our grown children.

I despise the moniker "gray." I think it denotes being drained of all vitality, and that certainly isn't me. I love dating in my 50s. Dating in my 20s was fraught with all sorts of impediments. It's no wonder I ended up in an unhappy marriage. I'm in a much better place now. —L.

As my 50th birthday approached, I decided my milestone was to get away from hair dye. Such a feeling of liberation!! I cut my hair short and just let it grow, kept chopping off the bottom. And slowly but surely, I was the real-hair me. And well, all I get is compliments—from men, women, and all ages too. Maybe now was good timing because with *Game of Thrones* and other people, celebrities and such, dying their hair gray, there's something trendy with the look. Sometimes, early in the changeover, I felt like people kept wanting to give me their seat on the Metro and I would look at them like, "How old do you think I am??" That doesn't seem to happen anymore.

AND, Laura, with the gray hair fully in place, I got on Hinge in January 2019 after breaking up with someone late in 2017 and taking 2018 off. I wasn't too sure if people would just be like, "Heck no, not that old, gray-haired person!" But it has been quite eye-opening. I have found that younger men don't seem to bat an eye, or maybe it's some mystique with MILF [Mother I'd like to f---] But I have gone out with quite a few men in their 20s and 30s. It's been quite fun and quite an adventure. And THEY reach out to me. —K. R.

PART I

SEEKING

CHAPTER ONE

~

My Big Fat Gray Divorce

A bird built her nest on the window ledge above our front door. Lex and I had been so preoccupied we didn't notice any activity until after we'd agreed to a very generous purchase offer. Our home hadn't even been on the market. A real estate agent with clients who were desperate to buy in our school district made cold calls on the Saturday before a holiday weekend. Neighbors who'd heard us talking about maybe, eventually, downsizing directed the agent to us.

Nest construction was completed during the week we entered and exited our home through the garage, to ensure the oil-based paint recoating the front door dried properly. We considered knocking down the nest, but then Linc and Sunny counted three eggs in it. The kids had climbed a ladder they'd set up inside our home for a look-see during a weekend visit to rummage through the big plastic bins we'd moved from our Richmond, Virginia, home a decade earlier. They excitedly unpacked, then carelessly repacked, treasures from their youngest years: Lego bricks, Barbie dolls, swim team ribbons, creatively spelled and vividly illustrated booklets.

The bird eggs hatched. According to Google, the helpless, tiny creatures needed a few weeks before they'd be ready to fly off on their own. Lex and I calculated this event would occur about twenty-four hours before our own move-out date. During the rare moments we were home together and sitting quietly, we watched the mother bird come and go, bringing food for the babies who shrieked at her absence.

If there was another meaning to the birds' presence beyond ironic metaphor, Lex and I didn't have the emotional energy to consider it. We were exhausted from packing up, throwing out, or tagging for storage an almost thirty-year marriage's worth of accumulations while crying, cursing, debating, and bargaining over what to do next.

Lex offered me temporary refuge in the condo rental he'd quickly found on Craigslist. I stared at him, tempted and also dumbfounded. "Do they allow dogs?" I asked. Lex reread the ad—nope. He called the condo owner to say the deal was off, then combed the website for a pet-friendly option. I clung to Lex's actions as though they had significance beyond his amazing capacity for denial.

Together, we checked out a different rental. The owners said we could bring our dog if we paid a nonrefundable pet fee as well as an extra two hundred dollars a month in rent. Lex was willing, but later, at home, I added a stipulation: The dog and I would join Lex if he put back on his wedding ring. He'd stopped wearing it a few years earlier, around the time he struck up a friendship with a woman he'd met at a conference. If we were going to live together even for a short time, I reasoned, shouldn't we at least embrace it as one last opportunity to see if we could work things out? You know, fake it 'til you make it. It seemed to me our long shared history, which included creating two humans, was a compelling reason.

Lex refused. Mona was just a friend, he insisted for the umpteenth time. Anyway, *she* was not the problem. The problem, according to Lex, was me. I was judgmental and jealous, trying to smother him and control his precious spare time. Lex had already left me once. He'd moved into a furnished rental shortly after we'd gone through the legalities of pounding out what was supposed to be a just-in-case property-settlement agreement, or PSA. We would turn it into a post-nup, Lex promised, if I would just shut up about Mona, finally learn to trust him, and basically leave him alone. I'd like to say I did just that. This is nonfiction, however, so I can't.

Nine months later, Lex returned home, saying he wanted to spend more time with Sunny as she completed her final year of high school. He stuck around after graduation and the year that followed. And everything between us was fine, just fine, as long as I didn't pound on the locked door of the extra bedroom in which he'd taken up residence or suggest we see a movie, go for a run, walk the dog together or interrupt his busy workday by calling to ask what time he would be home and would he be hungry for dinner.

Now, with this unexpected lucky break of a house sale, Lex said he didn't necessarily want to get divorced. But he needed his privacy, and he needed his space, and what was the point of putting his wedding ring back on when he didn't feel like we were married? Still, the dog and I were welcome to crash with him for a week or so until I could get my own place.

Thus, in the frantic hours before going to closing, I finally grew a backbone. I found a two-bedroom apartment in a brand-new building in the still-under-development Mosaic District. I paid a premium to sign the shortest lease possible: nine months. Surely Lex would have had all the privacy and space he needed by then.

Clearly, Lex was not the only one with an amazing capacity for denial. My nine-month lease stretched into more than two years of renewals and sadness, anger, anxiety, frustration, and flat-out scared shitlessness. Lex and I saw each other frequently; we'd have dinner with the kids or on our own. His company's health-care plan offered a much-needed safety net when my full-time proofreading gig was eliminated; if we got divorced, I'd lose coverage. Lex still wasn't in any hurry to make our split official, but that didn't mean he wanted to be my husband.

Gradually, I was able to discern the difference. I learned to let go of one full life lived so I could embark on another, solo. I read. I wrote. I ran. I tried yoga and meditation. I took my wedding dress out of storage and burned it in my apartment's kitchen sink. I landed a full-time editing job, with a health-care plan. I legally returned to my childhood last name. I bought a townhouse. I filed the divorce papers.

As I packed up my apartment, my mind wandered to the nest that a bird built on the window ledge above the front door of the house where, once upon a time, I'd been part of a we. Had it been some sort of sign? Hope is the thing with feathers, Emily Dickinson wrote. Poet Jack Gilbert noted that the Greek god Icarus melted his wings when he flew too close to the sun but still, he flew.[1] And Bob Marley sang of three little birds perched by the doorstep, singing sweet songs of melodies pure and true. Their message? Every little thing is gonna be alright.[2]

⟨◈⟩

Dear Laura,
Your introduction in the latest episode really stopped me in my tracks. . . . You mentioned your shame and embarrassment about getting divorced. . . . It resonated with me. I'm the youngest of five children—the "prob- lem" child, the "passionate" child, the one that always has to do things differently. When my wife left me, I felt sadness, anger, confusion, and, most of all, embarrassment and shame. Life seemed brutal and relentless.

This all went down in mid-December. We lived in a different state from my siblings, so I made up an excuse for why we weren't coming for the holidays. The prospect of letting them know the truth was so overwhelming and humiliating, I wanted to keep it a secret for as long as I could.

Then, the Sunday after New Year's, my dad called. Spending all day Sunday on the phone with the five kids, one at a time, had been my mom's thing. But she had passed about ten years earlier, and my dad had taken up the tradition. I was dreading this call because I knew I had to tell Dad my marriage was over.

Dad didn't say, "It's for the best—she's crazy!" He didn't say, "Don't worry, it's going to be okay"—which I hated hearing because it wasn't okay; my family was coming apart!

My dad just said, "I'm so sorry. What do you need from me?"

I told him I just needed someone to talk to, because I was feeling lonely and overwhelmed. So my dad stayed on the phone with me for two hours. This was really something, because Dad was a man of his times. Discussing feelings and vulnerabilities wasn't necessarily some- thing he felt comfortable with.

This memory came back to me so vividly. All of the emotions I was feeling at that time were suddenly so present and raw. Why am I telling you all this? I don't know. I just needed to share, I guess. Thank you for being so candid and honest about your experiences. —J. C., Michigan

⟨◈⟩

Laura,

Your podcast seemed to find me at just the right time. Been married thirty-two years, but just after the thirty-one-year mark discovered my husband's affair with a much younger work colleague with whom he travels extensively. It's been sixteen months of insanity and discovery as I learn more about the man I was married to, whom everyone who knows us would say [is] the last guy in the world they would expect this from. In any case, I moved out on my own. I've started a new career as a part-time consultant. Still, it feels like my entire identity was wrapped up in my kids and my family and is where I made most of my friendships—and that's largely gone. It's tough to wake up and realize your entire social circle is composed of married couples.

It's comforting to know there are others out there coming out of very long-term marriages and starting anew with optimism and renewed energy for life. —R., Maryland

Dear Laura,

I am fortunate that I "divorced well." I have rental-property income and lifelong spousal support that are enough to keep me pretty comfortable. I feel like men are always trying to size me and my situation up. For the most part, I was a stay-at-home mom, so I don't have some great career or full-time job that men can put a label on. They try to get bits of information without being too invasive. I get it. I want to be with someone who is financially compatible with me, too. —K. P., California

From season 1's "Things We Do For Love" episode, the following is an excerpt of my interview with journalist and author Steven Petrow. I asked him, postdivorce, what he was doing to find a new partner.

STEVEN PETROW: So, I have these two very good friends, and they had met through this matchmaker. And so when I started talking to this matchmaker, he explained to me some of his theories—which, if I remember correctly, were [that] we don't always know what we're seeking.

ME: Do you remember what your parameters were, that you thought you wanted?

STEVEN: My previous primary relationship had been with a writer, and all of my other boyfriends had been writers and . . .

ME: Oh, those creative types.

STEVEN: Creative types. And I did not wind up with that through Dale, who was the matchmaker. [My now ex-husband] was actually a real estate agent who had retired, was definitely not a creative type, not what I would have set out after. And so that sort of counterintuitive intelligence of the matchmaker really, yeah, brought us together and brought us together for fourteen years overall.

ME: How old are you?

STEVEN: How old am I in real life, or how old am I online?

ME: Oh, okay! [Laughter]

STEVEN: I have two different ages. I'm sixty-two as I sit here and speak to you. But on Tinder, I'm fifty-eight.

ME: Why are you younger on Tinder than you are in real life? And I'm asking this as someone who [has] never understood why people aren't upfront about their age. If you're not getting older, that means you've died. So what's there not to embrace about the beautiful sixties?

STEVEN: It's taken me a little while to embrace the beauty of my sixties. On Tinder and some of the other apps, when I'm setting age parameters, I tend to use round numbers. Like, forty to seventy. So my thinking was, if I come in a hair under sixty, I will not be excluded from those who are looking for roughly that age.

And so on first dates, I'm always very upfront about saying, "I'm not fifty-eight; I'm sixty or sixty-one." But I will say, Laura, I was chatting with a guy on Tinder, and we had exchanged last names. So he Googled me, and he knew some of what I had written—and he knew my real age. And he said I was being dishonest and that was a reflection of my values and that he didn't want to, you know, pursue this any further.

ME: I also have to be devil's advocate, I guess. Forty? I mean, that seems awfully young. So I was told that you should go ten years either way. But now that I'm almost fifty-nine, forty-nine even sounds young to me. So to go to anything younger than forty-nine—okay, you tell me. Uh, can you see yourself, uhhh . . .

STEVEN: I'm going to let you stew on that.

ME: [Laughter] Can you see yourself . . .

STEVEN: Laura, they're only numbers. They're only numbers. You know, I have been meeting and dating all sorts of people, all sorts of careers, lifestyles.

ME: And what are you looking for? Are you looking for, just to go out? Or are you looking for another committed relationship?

STEVEN: Overall, I'm looking for another committed relationship. But as a friend of mine says, not every date needs to go on that same road. So some might not be committed-relationship material, but they might be really nice or fun people. I'm an optimist. I'm on four dating sites.

ME: Wow.

STEVEN: I take introductions from friends . . . and recently I've been working with a new matchmaker. I'm trying to use the tools that are available to me.

CHAPTER TWO

~

Simon Says

The wind blew the fountain in Lake Anne sideways, spraying Santa and his reindeer as they floated by on a party barge. Santa's elves, in kayaks and canoes, wobbled in the rippling water but managed to steer wide of the fountain shower. The jolly man and his crew had arrived from one end of historic Lake Anne in Reston, Virginia, to the plaza at the other end, continuing the early December tradition of ushering in the start of the holiday season.

It was my first Christmas in Reston. I'd moved there a few months earlier, the same week that Robert E. Simon, the town's founder, had died, at the age of 101. As I learned more about Bob and my new hometown, it seemed fitting to me that I was starting the second half of my life in Reston. Bob Simon was many things: Harvard graduate and World War II veteran, real estate mogul, visionary developer. Above all, though, Bob seemed to me a role model for making meaningful personal connections at all stages of life.

Bob's first marriage lasted twenty years, ending when sadly, his wife died. About a year later, he married a woman named Anne and then about a year after that, in March 1961, Bob made a fateful real estate decision: Looking for a tax shelter for proceeds from his family's sale of Carnegie Hall in New York City, he purchased almost seven thousand acres of Virginia farmland.[1] This prime location was twenty miles west of Washington, D.C., and six miles west of the soon-to-be-dedicated Dulles International Airport.

Bob's intent was to create a special community with this land: a new town development. New town developments had started springing up in Europe in the late 1940s. Bob was among the first to introduce the concept to the United States. He didn't want another suburban neighborhood that people emptied every weekday morning for grueling commutes into the city. He envisioned a community where people of all ages, income levels, and—perhaps most radical for the time—races came together to live, work, and play.[2] He used his own initials to create the town name, R-E-S-ton.

Bob's master plan called for seven villages surrounding a central town center. Each village would have its own village center, accessible to residents by foot along paths and sidewalks. Shared community spaces would connect Restonians to recreation, nature, and each other.

In June 1962, the Fairfax County Board of Supervisors gave Bob's monogrammed community the green light. Three years later, in December 1965, Lake Anne Village opened. The architecture writer for the *New York Times* called it one of the most striking communities in the country.[3] Bob named it after his second wife, Anne. (How romantic!) Modeled after Italy's coastal town of Portofino, the anchor of Lake Anne Village Center was Washington Plaza. This main public-gathering space was lined with townhouses and low-rise buildings featuring living spaces above businesses including a pharmacy, library, beauty salon, restaurant, community center, and food market.[4] Outdoor sculptures on the plaza invited children to climb and explore them. The plaza opened onto the thirty-acre artificial lake, and the wooden Van Gogh footbridge linked the plaza to nearby housing clusters. Heron House, a fifteen-story concrete condo building, towered over the lake and served as the village center's focal point.

In May 1966, a splashy dedication ceremony for Lake Anne Village drew Restonians and local officials. Also in attendance were the Virginia governor, two U.S. cabinet secretaries, and guests from all over the world including architecture professors and students, and representatives from more than twenty countries with new town developments, such as Finland and France.[5] During the celebration, a telegram from President Lyndon B. Johnson was read aloud; the president congratulated

Bob for creating "a new town . . . which invigorates our concepts of urban planning." Bob also received the inaugural Urban Pioneer Award from the secretary of Housing and Urban Development. Then Stewart Udall, Secretary of the Interior, announced the federal government would soon break ground nearby for the U.S. Geological Survey's new headquarters.[6] Bob's vision of live-work-play Reston was becoming fully realized.

"Most prospective homeowners say 'Good,' when they hear that the community is not segregated, for people who move to Reston are not running away from anything," Ebony magazine reported. "They are hunting for an ideal community where their children can mature under the best circumstances while their own recreational and cultural needs are satisfied. They accept anyone who is trying to achieve the same goals in a congenial atmosphere. . . . Despite its Southern location, Reston . . . is a new kind of community that offers an exciting way of life for families, regardless of race."[7]

Yet only months after the dedication ceremony, Bob was removed from any further development of Reston. "In the American Dream, even Camelot has to break even," the Saturday Evening Post wrote. "And as of last fall, Reston had 2,700 residents and a debt of $45 million. To protect its own $15 million investment, the Gulf Oil Company took control of the limping Utopia, fired its founder and put the whole tangle into hands of . . . a real-estate consultant from Pittsburgh."[8]

Perhaps racism caused would-be buyers to stay away. Or maybe it was merely discomfort with making a personal investment in an untested concept. Bob retreated to the Big Apple while a new team took over. They modified his plans, eliminating two of the seven planned villages and eschewing the expertise of noted architects and visionary planners with European inspiration. The Tall Oaks, Hunters Woods, South Lakes, and North Point villages sprang up with considerably less finesse, their centers designed as strip shopping centers with surface parking lots instead of walkable plazas.

Still, Reston maintained character: two golf courses, three additional lakes besides Anne, and miles and miles of paved paths and trails through woods and open green space. In 2008, Reston made U.S. News & World Report's list of the "best healthy places to retire."[9] During the COVID-19 pandemic, Money analyzed about two thousand cities in the United States in search of "the best places to live if you work from home." Staff looked not only at sufficient Internet connection and space for all family members to comfortably work and distance learn from home but also ease of access to restaurants, pharmacies, and green spaces. Towns in Pennsylvania, Colorado, and California made the final cut, but Reston was number 1.[10]

While his namesake town was growing, Bob was living in New York—"lonely, depressed, and longing for the community he sought to create in Reston," according to those who knew him best.[11] When he finally returned to Reston to live in the early 1990s, he was eighty years old and long divorced from Anne after an eleven-year marriage. In fact, his third marriage of several years was on the rocks.

Bob settled into a spacious unit on the top floor of Heron House. He spent his days strolling around the lake he'd named in happier marital times. He was never too busy nor too preoccupied to greet passers-by and pose for photos. One day, he was in his building's elevator, on his way down to Washington Plaza for a walk. Also on the elevator was one of his neighbors. As Bob told a documentary filmmaker, he noticed his neighbor was wearing sneakers. He introduced himself and asked her if she'd care to join him on his stroll. She said yes, "and the rest," Bob said, "is history."[12]

Eventually, Bob and his walking partner and neighbor got married. When the couple wasn't traveling around the globe, they were enjoying their hometown, where Bob served as icon, senior statesman, and head cheerleader. By all accounts, he enjoyed fairly robust health. His death after a brief illness made national headlines and sparked an impromptu memorial gathering on Washington Plaza. Bob's birthday is marked every year in Reston with the Founder's Day celebration.

I moved to a townhouse cluster about a mile along a path to the public-access ramp for Lake Anne. About a mile in the other direction, the path hugs Wiehle Avenue as it leads to Isaac Newton Square. This was the former location of the "monkey house," a quarantine center for primates imported to the United States for use in research labs. In the fall of 1989, dozens of primates inexplicably got sick and died gruesome deaths. Turned out they had a form of the highly contagious and deadly Ebola virus. Thankfully, that strain wasn't harmful to humans. Eventually, all the monkeys were euthanized, the facility was abandoned and then torn down, and the monkey illness was named Reston virus.[13] The community drama in the following years has been much tamer, so to speak, involving residents perpetually battling greedy developers eyeing Reston's two golf courses with new housing developments in mind.[14]

I believe Bob himself would have been pleased at how quickly I felt at home living in the town he created. I jogged the paths and trails with the Reston Runners. I attended services at the Unitarian Universalist Church—in person before the pandemic and then over Zoom. I met a lot of people. None of them knew who I used to be. I also swapped stories with other gray daters; everyone had a tale to tell. I heard Clyde's after I signed up for Reston Association–sponsored pickleball lessons. Now sixty-five, Clyde had a long first marriage that ended in divorce and then a short second marriage that also ended in divorce. After the second split, he retired at age sixty-two. "I bought a minivan, put my golf clubs in there and some clothes and stuff for all seasons, and I hit the road," he told me.

Clyde spent the next two years traveling around the United States, playing golf and clearing his head, until February 2020. The pandemic convinced him he should return to Virginia, where he had siblings, grown children, and grandchildren nearby. "I decided I really liked Reston, with the paths and all the activities and, you know, biking and getting to D.C. You can hop on the Metro and get to D.C. very easily," he noted. "So, yeah, I decided Reston's the place for me for retirement."

Clyde settled into a townhouse on Reston's South Side. "I was at peace with where I was and thinking, *You know, if I'm single for the rest of my life, it's all good,*" he told me. But as fate would have it, he didn't stay single for long. In pickleball class he met Trish, sixty, whose long marriage had recently ended after Trish discovered her husband had been wildly unfaithful. Trish was also Clyde's neighbor. Over long walks and games of pickleball, they struck up a friendship that developed into something deeper.

"I was pretty happy before our pickleball class started," Clyde told me with a grin. "I'm really, really happy now. I feel like one of the luckiest guys in the world—better than if I hit the lottery."

Another Restonian I met, Van, is a retired Army officer and divorced father of six. Now in his early sixties, Van was still on active duty and working in the Pentagon on 9/11 when a plane hijacked by terrorists deliberately flew into the building. The force of the impact knocked him out of his desk chair and into a wall. His physical injuries exacerbated emotional injuries from combat deployments in Bosnia and other hellish locations. In the ensuing years, Van went through some dark times. Concerned friends intervened, and he eventually got help for post-traumatic stress. He earned a second master's degree, in pastoral counseling, and then a PhD. Today he's a therapist who helps military veterans and their loved ones.

Van was married for about sixteen years. He's been divorced longer than that. He didn't really start dating again until he was in his mid-fifties. He thought it was important to become emotionally healthy before attempting to deal with the natural ups and downs of romantic relationships. In the past twenty years or so, he had two such entanglements. Both flamed out. Perhaps the third would be the charm.

Van dated Girlfriend Number One for about a year and half. A busy professional, she was content to spend only Saturday evenings with him, he told me. Van wanted more, and they broke up. A few months later, Van met Girlfriend Number Two. They dated for several weeks and then, shortly before the holidays, she broke up with him. After the holidays, she reached out again. He responded and on this go-round, they dated for about a year.

Van thought Girlfriend Number Two would be the One, Only, and Forever. He was stunned when she inexplicably sent him an email saying she thought it would be better to be "amazing friends." Van was desperate for an explanation. He asked if they could discuss it with the help of a therapist. She agreed, but then things kept coming up in her schedule, and Van decided he didn't care anymore. Months later, she approached him after a memorial service for a mutual friend who'd lost his battle with cancer. She told Van she wanted to talk, but he declined.

Van understood intellectually that GF2 wasn't right for him. Still, rejection stung. And boy, did it hurt. When we spoke, he couldn't talk about her for long before choking up. All couples have disagreements, he knew that. It was the coming back together after the arguing that was so difficult. Van hoped the next woman he gave his heart to would want to work with him on healthy ways of communicating. He decided whoever his next partner would be, they'd attend couples therapy regularly.

Meanwhile, romance-wary Van was working on himself and learning how to communicate better. He earned his certification as a mindfulness-meditation instructor and talked a lot about not looking forward or backward but being in the moment.

This reminded me of something I'd read in Norman Lear's memoir, *Even This I Get to Experience*. At this writing, the legendary television producer and activist is still going strong at age ninety-nine and is in the third decade of his third marriage. Back in the day, though, he was ahead of his time, gray-divorcewise. After a brief first marriage, he wed Frances in the mid-1950s. When they split up thirty years later, his $100 million–plus settlement to Frances made headlines. In his 2014 memoir, Lear recounted turning to meditation later in life. He described living in the moment as the struggle to stay in the hammock slung between Over and Next.[15]

I loved that visual. But sometimes when I was sprawled diagonally in the queen-size bed I'd gotten in the divorce, I couldn't help but wonder if being single would be a temporary or permanent state. Not that I hadn't had company in my bed—though on many nights it was four-legged and furry. My sweet old pup had died of a broken heart about a year into my apartment rental. The veterinarian attributed it to age and disease, but I suspected there was more to it than that. I waited six months before adopting Jade, a mutt with the body of a golden retriever and the high-strung temperament of a terrier.

Jade and I both relished our warm weather walks to Lake Anne Village Center. Sometimes we took the path past the boat launch and through the woods. Other times we went the long way, down North Shore Drive and through a parking lot to reach the plaza. There, Reston founder Bob Simon relaxed eternally in the form of a life-size bronze statue.

Bronze Bob is seated on a bench. One arm rests in front of him, hand on knee; the other drapes the back of the bench. He wears a turtleneck and cap, and his bearded face is gleeful. It's as though he can't wait for me to experience everything he discovered about romance and love in the later years of life.

⌒∞⌒

From season 1's "Flying Solo" episode, the following is an excerpt of my interview with certified life and relationship coach Amy Schoen. I asked Amy about taking the first steps toward finding love again.

AMY SCHOEN: You need to get a real clear vision of what you want in your life, because different people want different things. You need to find a partner who's going in the same direction.

The second thing is, the values need to be aligned—what you want and what you think is important. What I find is that most people don't have a concrete sense of their values and a way to communicate them. And they're actually going after the wrong things.

ME: You would have me envision what I want . . .

AMY: For your life. I want to know what you want for your life [so you can] communicate that, whether it's online or verbally.

ME: Okay, so I would figure that out. And do I write it down?

AMY: There are exercises I take my clients through, yeah. My process is, first, really getting clear about who you are and what you want in a relationship and who's a good partner for you. The second step is, how do you put yourself out there? We have the whatnots at this age. *I'm not* . . .

ME: *. . . as successful as I want to be.*

AMY: Right.

ME: *I have problems with my kids* . . .

AMY: Whatever. Those are the gremlins. So, say what you do have to offer. You have a heart. You're a giving person. And then we take that information, and we sprinkle it into your [online dating] profile.

ME: [Dating is] hard. Isn't it?

AMY: Well, that's a perspective. What would be a different perspective that you would want to take on?

ME: Well, I would want to take on the perspective that it's easy, but experience tells me it's hard.

AMY: Well, how can you enjoy the journey? What would make it fun for you? I was at a point where I was like, "Are you the one? Are you the one?" I mean, I was driving myself crazy. And then I got an aha. I was like, *I'm just going to enjoy my life. I'm not going to stop trying, but I'm going to enjoy my life.*

My clients are intentional, and they don't give up. But they also learn to relax a little about the process. And when you relax, I think you draw in people, and you don't repel people.

ME: Repel people—that's interesting. What would I do that would actually repel someone?

AMY: Well, my belief is, if you're serious and you're looking for a serious relationship and the guy isn't and he runs away, let him. The right people will be attracted to you. The wrong people aren't.

ME: Ah, okay.

AMY: I like to see how dating is fitting into your whole life. So, one of the questions I could ask you is, what are your top three priorities in the next three to six months?

ME: Uhhhhh. My personal . . . well, are they . . . okay, this is terrible, because I'm, like, parsing every word. The realist in me says it would be really hard to find somebody, a committed partner, in three to six months. I would like to get on the path to finding a committed relationship.

AMY: My clients come to me when they're really ready to make space in their lives for this and this is becoming top of mind. And so my question to you—I mean, if a guy met you right now, how ready would you be for that relationship?

ME: Oh, totally ready. Totally ready. I am.

AMY: And how much time could you give a relationship?

ME: I'm pretty busy. But my philosophy, my attitude has always been, you make time for the people who are important to you. And so I would make the time. I would.

AMY: And how would you communicate [that] to that person? Because they're seeing you as a very busy person. Actually, my story is, my husband met me; we had one date, and he never asked me out for another date.

ME: What?

AMY: Yes. Five years later, we meet up again.

ME: Oh.

AMY: He perceived me as being too busy for a relationship.

ME: It sounds like the fact that I'm having so much trouble answering these questions . . . says something deep and, at the same time, shallow about me.

AMY: No, I think what it is, is really getting clear about what you want for your life and what does that look like, and how you can make space for somebody in your life. I had a feng shui consultant [tell me], "You don't have space for a man in your life. You need to clean out a closet"—that kind of thing. Do you have space for a man in your life right now? That's the question I'd like to leave you with.

Dear Dating While Gray:
I'm 63 and retired by default. Divorced after thirty-two years and moved to another state. Bought a single-family house. Connected with an old friend six months later and gave him a set of keys, then fell in love and found out he was in love with someone else who loved someone else. I sold the house and moved back to my previous state. Now I'm really alone. I just listened to your podcast and heard the life coach ask if you have room for a serious relationship, and my answer is yes! I had an entire house; it made no difference.

I do know the type of guy I'm praying for. I don't want to meet him online. I want him to see me and say, "I have been looking for you my entire life." —S. H., Virginia

Hi Laura,
There are so many things that stop me from dating—being annoyed [by] texting to start the conversation, worry about having sex after so long, my things. You know. And also that I'm not legally divorced yet although my husband has been in prison for five years (divorce papers are printed and I'm decided, but I have been something of a bleeding heart wuss). I want to organically meet someone; we're all off the hook for that at the moment. —L., Washington, D.C.

Just started listening, and I love your show. I'm a 66-year-old divorced Black woman and look probably about 45–50. I have started dating just as the shutdown started, went to the park as a date. Have been talking and texting. Not sure where to go from here. I really like the man I'm dating; he's divorced and 62. So nervous about this relationship; just want to enjoy it. LOL, just had to say it out loud. But I haven't been with a man other than my ex in over forty-five years. I'm nervous. Not sure what to do. —MPH

CHAPTER THREE

~

All the Good Ones

I was usually the ready-fire-aim type. But before I dove into the gray-dating pool, I wanted to attempt to measure how deep and wide it was. So I turned to the U.S. Census Bureau's most recent annual population survey. This report reliably offered a treasure trove of information, including how many Americans in specified age groups were married and not married.[1]

The married subcategories were "spouse present" and "spouse absent." Legendary public radio personality Diane Rehm is a statistic in the "spouse absent" column. She lives in Washington, D.C., where she hosted a weekday WAMU-NPR news program for more than twenty years. After retiring, she'd gone on to host the weekly podcast *On My Mind*, where she brought on politicians, artists, and authors, among others, to discuss—well, whatever was on her mind.

Diane had married for the first time when she was nineteen. About three years later, she got divorced.[2] Her second trip to the altar, with John Rehm, lasted more than fifty years. During the last nine years of their marriage, John suffered from Parkinson's disease and made the decision to end his life by refusing to eat, drink, or accept medication.[3] After he died, Diane told me for *Dating While Gray*, she never expected she'd find another romantic partner. (Dating, it seems, was not on her mind. Har-har.) But then an old acquaintance—another John!—

reached out. He was a retired pastor who lived in Florida. John and Diane embarked on a long-distance romance before deciding to have a long-distance marriage. "I'm not moving to Florida, and he is not moving to Washington; it will be a modern marriage in the most modern sense of the word," Diane said.[4] They became part of the *living apart together* trend, which I explore in chapter 10.

The Census Bureau population survey's other relationship categories were "never married," "separated," "divorced," and "widowed." I counted the people populating all of these categories as not married and, thus, potential swimmers in the gray-dating pool (although, as you'll learn in chapter 5, "separated" is a potentially tricky status from a dating standpoint). The not-marrieds aged fifty to eighty-four added up to slightly over 39 million. In comparison, almost seventy million Americans aged fifty to eighty-four were out of the water and living in Married Land, with or without their spouses.

Clearly the not-marrieds were outnumbered but wow, millions of gray daters, right? Not necessarily. The survey wasn't designed to specify how many of those 39 million were seeking same-sex partners and how many were seeking opposite-sex partners. Nor did it parse out those who weren't interested in dating at all. Denny, for example, was in his late fifties and had been separated for a few years when I chatted with him. The Northern Virginia resident had no plans to either divorce or date. He was a small-business owner who worked as many hours as he wanted and then rode his bike whenever he wanted. He seemed convinced that he'd get back together with his wife even though, shortly after their silver wedding anniversary, she moved out of the home where they'd raised their kids and bought her own place nearby. Denny was left with the family dog and another mortgage to pay.

Then there was Lisa, a fifty-seven-year-old Pittsburgh resident who had been single since her divorce twenty years earlier. "I can't really understand why everybody feels like I'm supposed to have a romantic relationship," she said when calling in to WAMU's nationally syndicated radio show *1A* during an episode devoted to finding romance later in life.[5] I was one of the guests that day.

1A's substitute host, Todd Zwillich, asked Lisa if she thought all men were useless, or was it only men fifty and older? "Let's put it this way," Lisa responded. "If I need repairs done on my house, it's far cheaper to hire a handyman than deal with the emotional toll that you get out of a bad relationship."[6]

Another single who also wasn't swimming in the gray-dating pool was Bella DePaulo. A social scientist at the University of California, Santa Barbara, she's the author of almost a dozen books, including *Singled Out: How Singles Are Stereotyped, Stigmatized, and Ignored, and Still Live Happily Ever After.*[7] Now in her early sixties, DePaulo has never been married. Moreover, since college, she's never been coupled or dated anyone seriously or even gone out on a date. Indeed, she has no romantic relationship goals, period. To each their own, I surmise. (Or maybe that should be, to each *on* their own.) As Bella told a TEDx audience in Belgium, she's devoted her career to shining a spotlight on policies and laws that favor married people, and debunking myths related to single people and unhappiness.[8]

I found another shortcoming of the census data, from a gray-dating-pool measurement standpoint: It didn't discern how many people in the not-married categories actually belonged in Married Land but simply lacked the legal documentation—in other words, folks who weren't married but were coupled. Take Kurt, a never-married whom I met through my running group. He had moved to Reston about a year before I had, by way of the Midwest, the South, and other map pins, tracing the route of his IT contractor career.

Kurt was five years younger than I am, but I thought he was in his forties. He was long and lean, and his hair was closely cropped but mostly still all there. His running pace was much faster than mine, but he would wait for me at the end of the Thursday-night group out-and-backs on the W&OD trail from the Reston Town Center's running store.

Kurt was sociable and sweet. Once he'd whispered with a wink that he liked older women. He talked even faster than I do—a rare feat!—especially when explaining his various inventions and licenses and patents. After exchanging cell numbers, we started meeting for dinner on nonrunning nights. Or we got our downward-facing dog on during the summer at free Sunday morning outdoor yoga at Lake Anne. We caught the late showing of *Get Out* one Saturday night at the Town Center cinema. Another weekend, Kurt replaced one of my

car's headlight bulbs after noticing it had burned out. I had been planning to just wait and get it done during the mandatory annual state
vehicle inspection that was coming up in a few weeks, but he couldn't
stop worrying about it.

Kurt had a high-pitched, endearingly goofy laugh. I heard it often
because he thought practically everything I said was the funniest thing
he had ever heard in his entire life. That was quite the aphrodisiac, let
me tell you. But as Kurt eventually, finally, revealed over a few beers
following a group run, he was more or less happily committed to his
live-in but frequently out-of-town girlfriend of about a dozen years. She
was also ten years younger than he was, which made her fifteen years
younger than I was. Apparently Kurt liked older women, but only up
to a point. Anyway, surely you picked up what I put down: Kurt was
single, but as for uncoupled? Not so much.

Back to the census data. It didn't reveal whether *not married* also
meant *uncoupled*, nor did it indicate interest and availability for being coupled and with which gender. But there were two facts that
could, indeed, be gleaned. Fact One: Women ages fifty to eighty-four
outnumber their male counterparts, regardless of marital status. Of all
people fifty to eighty-four years old, almost 53 percent were women,
compared to about 47 percent men. Fact Two: The percentage of older
women to older men grew more lopsided when looking specifically at
the not-married categories of separated, divorced, widowed, and never
married. Of all those not-marrieds ages fifty to eighty-four, 61 percent
were women, compared to 39 percent men. (Interestingly, among the
never-married people ages fifty to eighty-four, men had the edge at 51
percent, compared to 49 percent women.)

But wait, there's more! If you looked at the not-marrieds only in
the two oldest age groups—seventy-five to eighty-four and eighty-five-
plus—73 percent were women, compared to 27 percent men. I wasn't
interested in any goodies among these oldies. Not yet, anyway. But because men were more likely than women to couple up or to die sooner,
among other factors, it was reasonable to assume the gray-dating pool
was majority female. From a competitive standpoint, this was sobering
news for those who, like me, were seeking older men.

One school of thought is that the numbers really don't matter because if you're single, you're a loser. I mean, there must be a reason why

folks are uncoupled at this age, right? It was like the gray-dating pool was Rudolph the Red-Nosed Reindeer's Island of Misfit Toys, where the plane couldn't fly and the boat wouldn't float, and the rag doll looked normal but apparently had low self-esteem.[9]

"It does seem that a high percentage of people—both men and women—who are single in this age group are single for a reason," emailed Kay, who described herself as a young sixty-four-year-old surprised to find herself in the dating pool once again.

Kay believes people our age are uncoupled because we are addicted to alcohol or drugs or have deep-seated issues preventing us from navigating healthy relationships. We "might possess a fear of intimacy or fear of commitment or perhaps have never learned how to participate in a mutually respectful dynamic," she wrote me. Presumably Kay wasn't counting herself in that description. Or me either, I hoped.

"I would love to have an equal in my life," emailed Dee, in her late sixties, who said she's been single for decades after a divorce. She describes herself as "still good-looking," along with being brilliant and successful. (I would also add confident—not that there's anything wrong with that.)

"Where are our guy counterparts?" asked Michele, a friend from college. She'd been married for almost twenty years and divorced almost as long when we met to talk for the podcast. She lives in Washington, D.C., where she runs a successful executive-coaching business. With men comprising about 60 percent of her clientele, Michele knows how to connect with the opposite sex. Moreover, she was always doing something fun, especially prepandemic. She had season tickets to Nats baseball games, attended concerts and plays at the Kennedy Center and author readings and lectures at indie bookstore Politics and Prose, and loved checking out new restaurants and bars.

Yet Michele hadn't had a date "in years. Years! When I'm making plans, I ask my friends, 'Do you have a guy that I could go with?' The response is always, 'No, but I know about forty single women.'"

But wait. Even though the odds are in their favor, a lot of older heterosexual men I've interviewed aren't exactly rejoicing at their supposedly abundant options.

"My dates haven't met my expectations," said Robert, an IT consultant in his early sixties. "I tend to attract financially needy women."

Robert had started dating again after the end of his twenty-year marriage. His two kids were still in high school when his wife, a legal editor a few years younger, left the family home for a nearby apartment. "I was floored," Robert told me, wondering if the timing had anything to do with a work promotion she'd just received. "We were bickering a lot, but we'd been bickering for years."

John, a university professor in upstate New York, had been married for twenty-nine years before his divorce. In the years since, "I've had essentially no success in finding someone I want to spend the rest of my life with."

Mark, who was sixty-eight when we met, was a state government executive before retiring. He'd been married twice and widowed twice. Since then, he's been on some blind dates. (Actually, I was one of them; more on that in chapter 7). He's also been active with online dating and various social activities, all in an effort to meet another long-term partner. So far, though, he's barely gotten past the first date. Now, he told me, "my basic philosophy is *High hopes and low expectations*." Still, he keeps trying.

"I do not like the idea of spending the rest of my life alone," Mark admitted. "Honestly, I do not like the idea. I don't like doing things alone. I don't like traveling alone—I've done it; I don't care for it. I don't like dining out alone—I've done it; I don't care for it."

In so many words, all of these people searching for romantic partners were saying what many of us were fearfully thinking: *All the good ones are already taken.* Perhaps we should keep in mind this little nugget from my real estate agent, Sherri: "All the good ones are *not* taken because you're a good one, and you're not taken."

Sherri markets herself as an agent with a brain as well as a heart, and it fits. She's an award-winning real estate agent licensed in all three initials of the DMV (the District of Columbia, Maryland, and Virginia). Her side gigs include Airbnb hosting several properties she owns, dressing up as Cinderella for little girls' birthday parties, and providing models costumed as 1960s-style flight attendants for corporate events at the National Air and Space Museum's Dulles Airport annex.

A child of divorce, Sherri is as religious as she is hard-working. She's also a model-thin blonde with big blue-green eyes. Yes, folks, even

Sherri had trouble finding a mate. She told me all about it during our house-hunting forays in Reston.

"I used to think all the good ones are taken. But I'm a good one, and I'm not taken." This was the opening line of Sherri's Christian Mingle profile. She'd written it in a last-ditch effort to get a ring on it.

"I realized that if I assumed I'd meet only idiots and leftovers, that's likely what I would attract," she told me. Her previous efforts on various online dating sites had yielded "one decent boyfriend, a psychotic pervert," and a few good men who nonetheless had been better fits in the just-friends category.

After praying on it, Sherri adjusted her attitude and wrote that "good one" line as part of a fresh profile. It quickly attracted the attention of a builder named Dave. He'd been married and divorced and then found Jesus and now felt ready to start searching for another wife. Sherri and Dave dated for a year and a half before getting married a few months shy of Sherri's fortieth birthday. Still married a decade later, Sherri may not be a gray dater (yet, if I'm being pessimistic or, perhaps, realistic). But her point about keeping a positive attitude, about ourselves and about others, resonates with me.

Still, I decided to ask professional matchmaker Leora Hoffman her take on the "good ones" view. I'd heard about Leora from a man I'd met at a pre-COVID speed-dating event near Washington, D.C. This was how that night had played out: Fifteen women ages fifty to seventy took seats on one side of a long table at an otherwise empty restaurant. Fifteen men in the same age range took seats on the other side of the table. The event host rang a bell, signaling us to start chatting it up with whomever was sitting across from us. After about five minutes, the host rang the bell again. The women stayed seated; the men got up and moved one chair over to start chatting it up with the next woman sitting across from him.

After each man had completed his five minutes with each woman, we all got up from the table and proceeded to the bar, the better to continue a conversation with anyone we thought might be a potential dating partner. Instead of sticking around, I scribbled my email address on a napkin and thrust it at the man who'd mentioned during our five-minute table encounter that he had a friend who was a professional matchmaker. I may have stuttered as I clarified that my email address wasn't for him but for her—you know, for research—and would he please pass it along? To his credit, he did.

Leora, who lives in Maryland, emailed me promptly. We agreed to meet in the Tysons Corner area, a convenient halfway point. Over happy hour drinks at the Ritz-Carlton, Leora told me she'd been in business for more than thirty years. She laughed when I admitted that everything I knew about matchmaking I'd learned from *Fiddler on the Roof*. Then I brought up the "all the good ones" question. Leora agreed with Sherri: all the good ones are *not* taken. Whew! However, Leora cautioned, when good men reenter the dating scene, they usually get snapped up quickly.

"What happens in our culture is, when a man is back on the market, the women just match him left and right," she told me. "The neighbor, the coworker, the sister—society, for some reason, wants to reach out and match a man, but the same doesn't often happen with women. It's so unfair."

Unfair: truer words . . . you know the rest.

"I believe a lot of the good men are going to get involved with somebody new in a fairly short period of time after coming back on the market," Leora continued. "I'd estimate three to six months. The challenge is to find men in that window of time."

Sounded ominous. Before I could get all worked up about it, she noted that there are exceptions, and she has firsthand evidence. Leora had a gray-dating story of her own, involving a "good one" who'd been on the market for many years before she'd met him.

Let's start at the beginning.

Leora, a native New Yorker, was a lawyer. So was her first husband. After the birth of their daughter, Leora wanted a better work-life balance. She gave up a demanding litigation position for part-time legal work with a government agency. "The job didn't suit my personality," she said. "But part-time legal work is so rare in Washington that I grabbed it."

Three years later, on maternity leave with their son, Leora was doing some serious career soul-searching when her sister telephoned. A psychologist in New York, Sis had been divorced for about a decade and wasn't having much luck finding love again. "This may sound crazy," she confided to Leora, "but I'm thinking about going to a matchmaker." That was Leora's light-bulb moment.

"I knew so many single professionals in the D.C. area who were having trouble meeting people," Leora told me. "And I've always had a knack for 'getting' people very quickly. I've had that energy, that karma, where even strangers felt they could trust me and would confide in me very quickly. So I have really good instincts about people, I'm an extrovert, and I'm a romantic. Those three elements made me think I'd be a good matchmaker."

With her husband's encouragement, Leora met with a start-up consultant, who advised her to do market research before switching careers. So Leora returned to the part-time law gig when her maternity leave ended and in her spare time explored the business of matchmaking. She also met with single men and women of all ages and backgrounds to develop a pool of people who would become her core group of clients. "I love connecting with people," she said. "To me, talking to a room full of strangers is a joy."

After a year, she quit the part-time job and began Leora Hoffman Associates. "The first two people I ever matched fell in love in twenty minutes and are still married today," she told me. But her continued matchmaking successes soon made the problems in her own ten-year union impossible to ignore.

"I got separated with a lot of trepidation," she said. "A matchmaker getting divorced? I thought it would kill my career. Also, I really did not want to break up my family. He was a wonderful father, but he wasn't the right partner for me. I felt like I had to be true to my convictions that I'd been sharing with my clients and in workshops and presentations. I had to practice what I was preaching."

The divorce was contentious and expensive. It dragged out for three years as Leora battled for custody of both children. "It wasn't an easy time for me," she said, "but I found that helping other people meet one another was the best therapy I could have had. Instead of dwelling on my own issues, I just focused on other people. I got great satisfaction from doing it, and my business took off like a rocket. Maybe people related to me differently, but it was the opposite of what I feared would happen."

Leora was thirty-nine when her divorce became final. She spent the next decade and a half finding partners for other people while looking for one for herself. "I found it challenging to meet men because I wouldn't tap into my client pool," she said. Still, she had a few long-term relationships, including one that almost led to marriage. She was engaged when her friend Mary told her about J. H., a business colleague and buddy of Mary's husband.

A forensic psychologist and amateur musician, J. H. had become a widower in his late fifties after his wife succumbed to a long illness. For a few years afterward, he couldn't even think about dating. But then, he decided to plunge back in. He threw himself a big party to celebrate his sixtieth birthday, hiring a New Orleans jazz band to supply the music, and asking friends and family from all over the country to join him. He let them know he was ready to start dating.

"Oh, you've got to meet J. H.," Mary had gushed to Leora after the party. "He's a classy guy with wonderful friends, and I really see him for you." But Leora was committed to her romantic partner and declined.

Meanwhile, J. H. ventured into the world of online dating. It didn't go well. He finally decided he was lucky to have been blessed with one great love in his life and he'd make the most out of being on his own. He took down his account.

Around the same time, Leora ended her relationship. "He was content to just stay engaged," Leora said of her former fiancé. "He couldn't move it forward; his commitment issues came to the surface. So one day I turned to him and said, 'You know what? I'm done. I don't need to wait. I don't need to put a gun to anybody's head. If you're not willing to make plans to have a life together—and by definition, that's what getting engaged means—then this is not for me.'"

Leora took a moment and then called her friend Mary. "All right," Leora told her. "I'm ready to meet J. H."

J. H. agreed to get together with Leora as a favor to his friends, but he wasn't expecting anything to come of it. This first date was supposed to be a quick meet and greet at a bar. They ended up closing the place down.

But it wasn't love at first sight, Leora said. "He's tall and very thin, and I was used to shorter, stockier guys. But it was just, *Wow, this is a quality man, and I can really have a conversation with him*. It was by far the best conversation I had ever had on a first date. I didn't know about the chemistry. I just thought, *Let me spend some more time with him and see where, if anywhere, this will go.*"

J. H., too, was cautious. Though they began seeing each other regularly, "He didn't touch me for several weeks," Leora told me. "He did not even take my hand, let alone kiss me."

Uncharacteristically confused about a potential partner and his intentions, Leora met with Mary and her husband. "I told them I thought J. H. was a really great guy, but I wasn't getting any vibes from him. I didn't know if he was just looking for a friend or what. And Mary's husband said, 'Leora, trust me. J. H. is not just looking for a friend. He wouldn't be investing this amount of time in you. But don't try and take the lead here. He's been through a lot. Be patient.'"

"Had I not gotten that piece of feedback, I think I might have blown it," Leora said. "I'm a strong personality, and I'm not big in the patience department. My tendency would have been to say to J. H., 'Hey, where is this going?' But I really liked him, and I understood more about him after that conversation with Mary's husband. So I just waited, and eventually he made his intentions known. And it just blossomed from there."

Leora and J. H. dated for about a year. Then, in a six-month time frame, they bought a house together, got engaged, sold their former residences, and planned a wedding. The bride was in her mid-fifties and the groom in his early sixties when they walked down the aisle.

"J. H. told me he wasn't just looking for a roommate; he wanted to be married," Leora said. "I wasn't exactly needing to be remarried, but I like the idea of marriage. I think it gives you a grounding. It's the ultimate commitment, and it was something I was very comfortable with doing again with the right guy."

Aww. Who doesn't love a gray-romance story with a happy ending? Maybe I sighed because Leora assured me my time would come. The right person was somewhere out there, she promised, or he would be soon. "There's always turnover," she said. "Sadly, people die, but that means their partners come back on the market. People break up, people get divorced; new people come on the market. There's a revolving door. So much of love is timing, but I also believe in fate."

⌒⌒⌒

From season 1's "Flying Solo" episode, the following is an excerpt of my interview with Dennis. He's in his late sixties and a lifelong New Yorker who recently relocated to be near family in Alabama. I met Dennis back in 2009, traveling throughout India as part of a group tour. Married and divorced twice, Dennis was a reluctant dater then and, as I discovered, still is.

DENNIS: The last serious relationship I had lasted about, I don't know, ten months. And I really do not date at all. I don't go online. Over the last ten, twelve years, I've been set up with probably six or seven blind dates by friends. All the women have been very nice and have had compatible interests, but there was no real chemistry.

I don't know if that chemistry is gone, but I saw no reason to follow up with a second date. I have a feeling that that part of my life is, you know, unless something comes along, I'm not looking for.

ME: When you say that you think the chemistry might be gone, are you saying you don't know if you're able to be attracted to anybody at this age?

DENNIS: No, not at all. It just is not important. I mean, certainly I'm lonely at times. I would love a companion to go to a show with, somebody to go to dinner, to travel with. But I'm not into the effort. I don't go to bars. I'm not going to go online.

And the activities that I do probably do not lend themselves to meeting people. I play bocce, I play ping-pong, I swim, I do yoga. And I actually do yoga at home; I'm not even in a studio. I do go on a yoga workshop for eight days in Costa Rica. It's mostly women. But again, they're not there for dating; nor am I.

ME: I talk to a lot of single women who say all the good ones are taken. How would you respond to something like that?

DENNIS: Well, I agree with them. I don't think there's many good men.

ME: Oh my god, Dennis, no!

DENNIS: I don't think that they're all gone. But I think it's harder to find a good man than a good woman.

ME: What do you think you might do if you wanted to get serious about finding someone?

DENNIS: If I wanted to, the easiest thing would be to go online.

Me: But you said you won't do that.

Dennis: Well, I haven't done it, and it's not something I'm contemplating. In two or three years, that might change. But you also become comfortable in your life. Even when I was dating Kellie back in '16 and '17, it affected my life. You know, you have to make compromises. And I was willing to do it because I thought she was great. [But] I didn't have freedom. I travel and do whatever I want, whenever I want. And when you get in a relationship, it's not quite as one-sided. That freedom is good. It's, you know, on a weekday night or Saturday night at seven o'clock after you've had dinner . . . you know, I'm left [alone] reading the New York Times.

Me: Yeah. Sometimes you get lonely?

Dennis: Yeah. Yeah. Certainly the majority of the time, I'm fine alone. But there certainly are times when it would be nice to, you know, cook someone dinner. And certainly there are times when you're lonely—times when you're everything.

Me: What do you mean, times when you're everything?

Dennis: I mean, there are times when you're happy or sad. You're mad, you're angry. Your life is filled with emotions. It's not one-dimensional in any direction.

Me: Do you think you can experience all that more profoundly on your own? Because everybody knows you can be lonely in a relationship too.

Dennis: Well, to me, if you're lonely in a relationship, you don't have a relationship.

Me: [Laughter] Okay.

Dennis: A lot of people settle, compromise. And . . . this is probably why I'm single. I always advise people not to settle and not to compromise. And so, you know, if you're lonely in a relationship, you don't have a good one. You want to be with someone very, very special. [Like Randi, a woman Dennis met after his first marriage ended. Randi also was divorced. They dated for about five months nonexclusively. Dennis stopped seeing Randi when he became serious with another woman.]
    I made a wrong decision, ended up marrying my second wife instead of Randi. [By the time Dennis and his second wife split up, Randi had remarried.] Then Randi and I had an affair for about nine or ten years.

ME: Oh!

DENNIS: I think she's perfect. And I sometimes think that before I die that we'll be together. I always think it might be when I'm ninety, and that means I've still got a long way to go.

ME: You think she's perfect. That makes me a little sad.

DENNIS: I shouldn't say *perfect*; there's no such thing as perfect. But she and I get along incredibly well. It's just completely easy. You know, we have a million things in common. It's the best relationship that I've ever been in. And from time to time, we speak and we text. If I ever see her name on the phone, my life just lights up. I just get excited.

ME: Awww.

DENNIS: You know, I'm not single and not dating because I'm waiting for her. I don't necessarily think it's going to happen. But, you know, who knows?

Hi!
I might be ready to head out to the dating world at age 61. I'm a pianist and really want to find someone to play jazz and Irish music with me. Gets worse because I would like a fiddler or a clarinet player! Can I be that picky? I also love to dance, so could he dance too? How do I stop obsessing over that? —C., Colorado

Hi, Laura . . .
It's frustrating to hear women say things like, "Why are all the good men taken?" I always want to wave my hands and yell, "Hey, I'm a great guy. I'm over here!" I'm affectionate, caring, kind . . . I like to snuggle with someone while watching a movie . . . cook for someone I love, have good conversations, and consider myself reasonably intelligent, a good listener, and a good cook. (As a bonus, I've also been told I'm a good kisser.)

[But] I . . . rarely get a second date, even when I feel like they went well and we had a connection. Most of the time I . . . never know why, although a few have given me reasons, including

- My salary isn't good enough.
- I currently can't afford to travel like they want to.
- I have cats (two). (Maybe I'm the male equivalent of a "crazy cat lady"?)
- They don't drink and I do (albeit usually just wine with dinner).
- I'm not a Christian. I'm an agnostic and don't believe in a personal god but respect everyone's individual beliefs.
- I'm a vegan.
- I'm not tall enough—only 5'8".

I fear I'm coming off as a whiner. I'm really not. I guess I wanted to show that it's not just women who are having a hard time. —S. J., Maryland

Laura, part of being single for me is learning how to live with just myself and not needing anyone to talk with (I'm separating "needing" from "wanting"). One of the benefits of remembering who I am is finding out that I'm a pretty neat guy, despite what I've been told the past few years. —N. K., California

CHAPTER FOUR

～

Star Signs and Wish Lists

After my Reston Runners friend Kurt confessed he had a girlfriend, he started looking around on my behalf for single men. One evening while he was out drinking with work colleagues, he texted me a photo of a man named Gary, taken and sent with Gary's permission. Kurt's text said he'd already shown Gary my Facebook photos, and Gary agreed I was pretty.

Gary was in his early sixties. He was a human resources manager at a big defense contracting firm where Kurt had his current consulting gig. In the photo, Gary was sitting at the bar, leaning forward to look directly at the camera. His tie was loose; shirtsleeves were rolled up. He sported a thin, feathery moustache, and his silver hair was brushed straight back and slightly parted. He was not unattractive, though I wasn't instantly gaga. The expression in his eyes seemed wary.

Kurt told me later that Gary was a nice guy, albeit a little quirky. But as Kurt described Gary, I began to think a more apt term might be *frugal*. (Not that there was anything wrong with that.) Gary had been working for the big defense contracting firm for many, many years, since getting out of the military after a short tour of duty. He was well dressed every Monday through Thursday; suits and ties were fairly time-less fashion. But on casual Fridays, Gary wore his acid-washed jeans from the '80s that—good for him—still fit. Sometimes he paired them with a caramel-colored pleather Members Only jacket.

Gary had squirreled away an unbelievable number of vacation hours so he could trade them for cash when he retired soon. His never wanting to dip below a certain threshold so he could treat his wife to a special, long getaway supposedly had nothing to do with their child-less marriage ending after twenty years. Still, it was over. Gary's wife stayed in their house for the requisite six months while waiting for the divorce to become final. (For a no-fault divorce in Virginia, childless couples and those with kids eighteen and older must be separated for six months. Couples with children under eighteen must be separated for a full year.)

Meanwhile, Gary set up camp at his employer's. No sense in fork-ing over any more money until absolutely necessary. For half a year, Gary slept for free on a cot in his office. He ate one meal a day, in the company cafeteria. He showered and dressed in the company gym after his workout.

When Gary was finally officially single, he bought a condo in the exurbs to sacrifice a decent commute for a low monthly payment. Ac-cording to Kurt, Gary hadn't dated much. No pressure, but would I be interested in attending the next company happy hour to meet him? *Sure*, I replied. *Why not?* I wasn't overly enthusiastic, because Gary didn't seem like my type in either looks or personal spending habits. But who was I to write someone off before I'd even met him?

The following week, I joined Kurt, Gary, and four of their cowork-ers at a rectangular table in a Northern Virginia sports bar. It was sort of like the speed-dating event I'd attended, except no one moved after five minutes. The bar was so loud we couldn't engage in a decent con-versation; it was Kurt, not Gary, who cheerfully insisted on buying the rounds. But Gary made a point of asking for my phone number and email address, and I gave him both. A day or two later, he reached out to ask if I'd like to go out to dinner. He'd make a reservation.

We met at Gary's appointed place and hour, settling in to peruse the menu and talk. Right away, Gary told me he's into astrology. Now, this may sound cheesy to you but for a moment, I thought this date might actually go somewhere. When I was very young, my otherwise sensible mother had introduced me to the signs of the zodiac via the daily newspaper's horoscope column. I was fascinated, and by the time I was in eighth grade I was thrilled to have landed a horoscope-writing gig of my own. My bylined columns for the Washington Irving school paper, *The Wisp*, consisted of insights I'd make up out of thin air, based on whom I had a crush on that week. (When you think about it, this may not be too far removed from how professional stargazers compose their own columns. Kidding!)

Actual horoscopes I wrote for *The Wisp* in June 1974:

Capricorn, the Goat: Your life has been awfully dull lately. Why not break up with your girlfriend or boyfriend? There are plenty of fish in the ocean, and you have pretty good bait!

Aquarius, the Water Bearer: Curb your harsh ways, and become the kind of person *everyone* wants to know! Remember, Aquarians are supposed to be humane, so start petting dogs.

Pisces, the Fish: You have become entirely too insulting. If you're wondering why people avoid you in the halls, now you know!!!!

I no longer write horoscopes. (I've also stopped using multiple exclamation marks.) But reading my daily horoscope? It's as habitual as brushing my teeth. Logic and intelligence notwithstanding, I hesitate to get going in the morning until I've learned how the upcoming hours are destined to unfold. True fact: On the day I was writing these words, my horoscope said, "This isn't a good day to go out, Scorpio. Traffic is probably awful." And what do you know? It was the Friday before a holiday weekend, so traffic probably *was* awful. I hadn't been planning to use my car that day because I was already happily holed up at a friend's farm for some focused writing. I was speechless, Horoscope. com. Just . . . wow.

Back to Gary. He said he was into sun signs. Same! Except, Gary continued, he had discovered via my Facebook page that I was a Scorpio, born in the Year of the Rat. (Apparently Gary liked his Western astrology mixed with a side of Chinese zodiac.) Somberly, Gary continued, he was a Leo, born in the Year of the Monkey.

Scorpio was a water sign, Gary explained—as if I didn't know—and Leo was a fire sign. Surely we would be doomed in all matters of romance because, just like that, my rat water would extinguish his monkey flame. Still, Gary said, because I was a water sign, I'd probably enjoy accompanying him on a cruise he wanted to take in early spring. The deposit was due soon; Gary was eyeing a room that cost more than he wanted to spend on his own. What did I think about splitting it? Gee, thanks, Gary, but I'll pass. We did split the dinner tab—no surprise—after he let the bill linger on the table until I finally offered up my debit card.

Here's where I confess: I long ago memorized which sun signs were supposedly the best matches for Scorpio: Cancer, Capricorn, Pisces, and Virgo. (Kurt's a Virgo, by the way. So's British actor Colin Firth. Just sayin'.) According to astrologer Leslie McGuirk, though, there is a lot more to determining romantic compatibility than comparing sun signs. As Leslie explains, one's sun sign is determined by date of birth. The time of birth and place of birth offer more insights about romantic pairings. Birth date, place, and time—astrologers put that information together to create what's called a *natal chart*. Evaluating natal charts for relationship chemistry is a centuries-old practice called *synastry*.

"When you're born, you're imprinted with a vibrational map, sacred geometry of where all the planets were at the moment of your birth," Leslie told me. That planetary alignment is your unique pattern, akin to the pattern of a snowflake. So it isn't enough to simply look for a compatible sun sign, because "It's not detailed enough." Here's what Leslie evaluates:

Moon signs: "Are these two people emotionally compatible?"
Mercury signs: "Can they communicate with each other?"
Venus signs: "Do they have sexual chemistry? Some people love to touch all the time. People who have their sexual energy in air, they hate that. It doesn't mean they're not great lovers or wonderful people. It's just, they have a different need. They're designed differently."

Leslie also told me that in her judgment, astrology "is one of the best ways to figure out whether or not someone is safe for you. There are some people who karmically are just not heathy for us."

In 2020, synastry went high-tech when a former Apple product-design manager named Rachel Lo launched a dating app called Struck. After users provided their birth date, place, and time, they were sent up to four potential romantic connections each day that were based on compatible natal charts. As a millennial mechanical engineering and materials science grad from U.C. Berkeley, Rachel might seem too left-brained to embrace astrology. But she told a *Los Angeles Times* reporter that not only has she been an avid user of dating apps, she also discovered mental and emotional benefits in her personal life after turning to astrology. Combining the two, then, seemed like a natural step. "In my life and a lot of people's lives, astrology coexists with science," she said. "They're not mutually exclusive contexts."[1]

Struck had barely gotten off the ground when it went out of business in 2021. Still, I'm with Rachel, and with Leslie, in believing that astrology's a fun, potentially insightful way to find a good romantic fit. Others disagree. Indeed, I've gotten some listener flak for even broaching the topic. "I can only say the following about astrology: what a load of crap!" commented J. A. This was on the *Dating While Gray* Facebook page post promoting the "Love in the Stars" podcast episode—before it had even been released. And though E. from Canada "enjoyed all previous episodes" of *Dating While Gray*, she used her one and only opportunity to rate the show on Apple podcasts with a mere three out of five stars: "Didn't like this episode. Not a believer."

In the interest of thorough research, I asked some gray daters about their nonastrological ways of discerning a good romantic fit.

"I'm an engineer, so I'm usually very specific about things," said Harry, a longtime resident of Fort Wayne, Indiana, who's in his mid-seventies. In matters of the heart, however, "You can't be too specific," he advised.

Harry married for the first time when he was only twenty. Seven years later, it was over. In an unusual move for the times, a judge awarded him sole custody of his three young children. Harry was juggling his engineering career and single fatherhood when he met a woman named Susie at a Fort Wayne ski club. They got married and had a daughter together. Eventually, Harry retired. He and Susie were looking forward to traveling and spending time with their children and grandchildren. After forty years of marriage, they still enjoyed each other immensely.

Then doctors discovered that the melanoma they'd all thought Susie had conquered had returned. Tragically, she had only weeks to live.

She bravely asked Harry to sit down for a heart-to-heart. "Susie told me I needed to go out and find another wife because I wasn't the type to live by myself," Harry told me.

Not that Susie was worried about Harry taking care of himself. "I cook, I do laundry, I sew, I clean house," Harry explained. "There aren't that many men my age who can say that. It's that she knew I'd be lonely and would want someone to share my life with."

Smart woman, that Susie. According to researchers, loneliness and poor health are linked. That's why finding ways to make and maintain interpersonal connections became important talking points when the COVID-19 pandemic confined us to our own homes. A prepandemic analysis of the health effects of social isolation and loneliness dug into more than two hundred studies involving four million people. The analysis found loneliness was as damaging to the health as smoking fifteen cigarettes every day and more damaging than obesity. It increased the likelihood of developing high blood pressure, heart disease, and stroke, among other ailments.[2]

Then there's the fear of dying alone, literally. *Elder orphan* is a term used to describe someone who's growing older and lacks a spouse, companion, or family member to call on for assistance. Researchers estimate that more than 20 percent of Americans older than sixty-five are elder orphans or at risk of becoming one.[3] The issue is particularly acute for single people who identify as lesbian, gay, bisexual, or transgender. They are less likely than non-LGBT singles to have adequate family-support systems in place to help, according to advocacy group SAGE.[4]

Japan, with the fastest-aging population in the world, counts approximately thirty thousand *lonely deaths* annually.[5] Lonely deaths occur when single people, usually men fifty and older, die alone in their homes. Their bodies often go undiscovered for weeks or even months. An entire industry in Japan has been built around cleaning up and sanitizing the spaces where these lonely deaths have occurred, to make them reinhabitable.

Turning to family members and friends could help uncoupled people avoid experiencing the social isolation that can lead to health woes and lonely deaths. But the outlook isn't entirely rosy for coupled people. Many experts predicted that confinement caused by the COVID-19 shutdown might lead to a rise in U.S. divorce rates similar to what

China experienced in March 2020 after its stay-at-home restrictions were first lifted.[6] (Maybe absence really *does* make the heart grow fonder.) China was the first country to go into lockdown, in January 2020. Also, a report out of India that left me feeling squeamish found an increasing number of unhappily married people chose suicide over divorce.[7]

Still, some research suggests that marriage itself offers protective health benefits. For example, a study in JAMA *Surgery* found that being married improved the chances of patients fifty and older recovering after cardiac surgery.[8] And according to an analysis in the *Journal of Neurology, Neurosurgery & Psychiatry*, the risk of dementia was lower for married people than it was for widows and widowers. It also was lower for married people than it was for people who'd never married. (Interestingly, researchers found no difference in dementia risk when comparing married people to divorced people.)[9]

Back to Harry. He told me that shortly after Susie died, he decided to start looking for another special someone. Three months after her funeral, he gingerly dipped his toes into the dating pool. His oldest three kids were supportive, but the daughter Harry had with Susie thought he was moving too fast. "She'd been very close to her mom, and it was a big loss," Harry said. "I understood that, but my attitude was, *Life can be taken away so quickly. I don't know how much more time I get. Maybe it's one year, maybe it's ten years. I'm not going to just watch the grass grow.*" Plus, Harry reminded his daughter, he had Susie's blessing to look for a new partner.

What exactly was Harry looking for? "I set some general guidelines," he told me. "I wanted a woman who was my age or younger, but no more than ten years younger. I'm only five-six, so I wanted a woman who was my height or shorter. And I didn't want a woman who was emotionally or financially needy. I knew that I was kind of a walking target, being retired and financially in good shape."

"I'm a healthy, high-energy guy," Harry continued, "and I wanted someone who could keep up with me. And I wanted someone who was a good traveler because I wanted to go places and do things."

With those parameters, Harry signed up with an online dating site. He spent about a year actively dating women throughout Northern Indiana, but he was feeling out of sorts in his home state. "At this stage of life, all of your relationships with friends change profoundly when one spouse is removed," Harry said. "It just wasn't the same."

So Harry decided to check out "snowbird" living, the slang term for Northern and Midwestern retirees who move to warmer Southern spots to live during the brutal winters back home. Harry traveled to Punta Gorda, Florida—he and Susie had liked vacationing there—and though his plan had initially been to find a place to rent, he wound up buying a condo. Even as a part-time resident, he got involved with the homeowners association, participated in community social activities, and found golf buddies. He also expanded his online profile search to Florida zip codes.

"The first week I was in Florida, I emailed fifteen women," Harry said. "Believe it or not, in six days I had dates set up with five of them. My haunting fear was that I would screw up and use the wrong name."

One of those women was Lani, a Filipina native ten years younger and more than six inches shorter than Harry. She had other qualities he found attractive. "She's a very hard-working person," he said, "and she's very neat." Harry was smitten from the get-go. Lani, twice burned in divorce, needed a little convincing before happily agreeing to a beach wedding on the Fourth of July. Harry sold his house in Indiana and now lives in Florida with Lani full time. "I made a whole new life for myself," he said.

Maxine's wish list for a partner might not be overly specific. Still, it could be considered a heavy lift. She wants someone with whom she can effectively communicate so they can smoothly navigate being in an open relationship. Monogamy didn't work out well for Maxine, who lived the first sixty years of her life as a heterosexual man, Max, and had married and divorced three times. Owner of a successful auto repair shop and self-described alpha male, Max's hobbies had included motorcycle and stock car racing and jumping out of airplanes. Still, Max had felt restless. "I'd get to the pinnacle, achieve what others couldn't, and go, 'Eh, this is nice. Let's go home.' Just kept searching and searching and searching."

Max discovered their true self during their third marriage, when they embarked on an affair with a woman who'd wanted to spice things up in the bedroom. She asked Max if she could dress Max up as a woman. Max agreed; "I was comfortable with my sexuality." But the girlfriend didn't have any clothes that fit Max, so they went online and met a woman selling designer castoffs who had connections to the trans community. "I went to her house, and I bought a bunch of stuff, and she said, 'Have you ever been dressed up?' I'm like, 'Nah, my girlfriend wants me to dress up.' She goes, 'Look, let's just make you up.' So I put the clothes on. She did my makeup, put a wig on, got me all fixed, and then turned me around so I could look in the mirror. And in that split second, that was the answer to every question I've ever had in my entire life."

Maxine told me she never looked back. "There's two scenarios," she said. "You either know at a very young age and you fight this all the way through your life, which is horrible. Or there's the [people] who later in life just sort of figure it out—like myself." Now Maxine, she finalized her divorce. Her girlfriend accepted the transition but moved out of state for work. Maxine realized that as a woman, she was still primarily attracted to women. She became involved with the trans community and also with polyamory. "It's the ability to love more than one person at a time, and it forms many levels [of partnership]," she told me.

Here's part of our conversation from season 1 of *Dating While Gray.*

MAXINE: Some are play partners. Some are committed couples that, you know, really have a deep love and connection and want to have some sort of life together. It gets complicated, because generally polyamorous couples wind up having other partners. I don't at the moment have another partner, but my girlfriend is married. She has another partner, and then her husband has, I think, three partners.

ME: I have a hard time with jealousy, so I can't even imagine dating more than one person at a time.

MAXINE: You have to embrace the term *compersion.*

ME: Compersion?

MAXINE: *Compersion* is a polyamorous word. It's when you are happy for your partner's happiness. I mean, I've asked my girlfriend many times, you know, she's been out with a date . . . spent the night. I'm like, "Hey, did you have a good time?"

ME: But you don't live together.

MAXINE: No, we do not.

ME: So you live by yourself. And you used a term . . . *nesting partner.*

MAXINE: Right. It's a description of the person you live with.

ME: Do you want a nesting partner?

MAXINE: I think so. I think I'm at a point in my life that my transition has gone, you know, along far enough to where I'm sort of settled into what it is. And I'm not a spring chicken anymore. And, you know, sometimes it's a little lonely.

ME: So what are you looking for in a nesting partner?

MAXINE: Somebody to have a deep connection with. It really has to be, you know, on that level, that trust, that you really care for [each other]. I'd say you really have to love them really well and deeply. It isn't really a physicality thing but, you know, generally really good lines of open communication where you spend a lot of time discussing a lot of stuff.

ME: That's really hard to do, whether you're in a polyamorous relationship or not. Communication is tough.

MAXINE: When you have two people—or three or four, whatever—who embrace polyamory and have studied it and understand the principles of it, discussion and compromise are a huge thing. And it tends to work out well.

ME: You find it easier?

MAXINE: Sure, because the person you're talking to is expecting you to go ahead and tell them things that they might not be comfortable with. And rather than blowing up and losing their cool, they're like, "Well, you know, that's a hard *no* for me. And I really, I can't go there. Let's discuss what we can work out."

ME: What's more important for you right now? Do you want to find a person to, you know, have a relationship with, and if they don't want to be polyamorous, would you be open to giving up the polyamorous lifestyle to be in a relationship just with one other person?

MAXINE: No, because it would be a lie.

ME: Okay.

MAXINE: I am not able to, honestly, be monogamous. And if the person expected that, that would be hurtful to them.

～✖～

Lucy, a graphic designer now in her early sixties, has also set some general guidelines for finding a partner. "A kind man would be good. Employed would be good, too," she said with a laugh, "or someone with a nice retirement fund."

Prepandemic, Lucy and I had met up at a Whole Foods grocery store that proudly advertised its outdoor happy hour. It was rockin' when we were there despite the cramped, fenced-in space having all the ambience of the parking lot and road it abutted. Lucy told me she'd never been married and then suggested I change the title of this book to something more on point—like *Profiles in Courage.*

Lucy has long been accustomed to making jokes about her romantic life, or lack thereof. When she was in her thirties, she and her apartment mate had irreverently set a low bar for the qualifications needed to win their hearts. They changed the message on their telephone answering machine, instructing single male callers to leave their name and number if they had "some semblance of hair, missing teeth have been replaced, and hands come clean when washed."

"My dad thought we were humiliating ourselves," Lucy said. "But you've got to laugh."

Lucy and her apartment mate lived together for five years. Then the mate clicked with a work colleague and moved to Married Land. Lucy stopped waiting for a husband to fulfill her dreams. She bought a townhouse; she adopted a child from overseas. She left her full-time job to freelance so she could help her child deal with learning disabilities and emotional-health issues. She hadn't had a serious relationship, much less a meet and greet, in almost twenty-five years. Then again, she hadn't put herself out there. Lucy had never tried online dating. She wasn't involved in activities that might give her opportunities to meet someone organically. Still, she had not given up hope that Mr. Right was somewhere out there. If this sounded unreasonably optimistic, the U.S. Census Bureau's population survey shows that the percentage of never-marrieds declines as people age.[10] One optimistic interpretation? We're never too old to get married for the first time.

Overseas, reports from Asia show that the number of South Korean brides and grooms fifty and older rose from 2017 to 2019, while the number of brides and grooms under age fifty sharply declined.[11] In Japan, the government's population survey no longer uses the term *lifelong singles* for people who reach age fifty without ever being married. The number of Japanese citizens who remain unmarried by age fifty has risen significantly, from under 5 percent in 1985 to about 23 percent for men and 14 percent for women in 2015.

At the same time, the number of Japanese getting married for the first time after age fifty is also rising. According to the National Institute of Population and Social Security Research, the number of Japanese men ages fifty to fifty-four marrying for the first time in 2015 was almost five times higher than that same cohort in 1990. For Japanese women in the same age range over the same time period, the number has approximately doubled.[12] Fun fact: In Japan, couples can choose to go with the bride's last name or the groom's last name, but the government requires married citizens to have a common surname, regardless of age at marriage.[13] (The government has long banned gay marriage, though in March 2021 one Japanese court ruled the ban unconstitutional.[14])

Back to Lucy. Despite years of singlehood, she refused to settle. "I want somebody in my life, but I don't want just anybody," she told me. "I didn't wait this long to take whatever I can find." Lucy joked about hoping to find a wealthy man but in all seriousness, financial independence is important to her. "I'm at an age where I don't have time for financial recovery," she said. "What I'll have in my retirement account ten years from now is what I'll have to live on for the rest of my life. When you get married young, you build assets together and have a long time to keep building them. And you don't have to worry about whose kids are getting what after you're gone."

She continued, "Even in a committed relationship at this age, you have to have your own money. You can't allow someone to have full access—or can you? I don't know. It seems complicated."

Lucy understands that most people fifty and older have "baggage," whether related to previous romantic relationships, kids, elderly parents, or something else altogether. "But you know how the airlines will let you carry on only so much? Well, that's my philosophy with men," Lucy said. "If your baggage doesn't fit, don't carry it on. Everybody has baggage, but it has to fit."

Lucy finished a French fry and then turned the tables. "How about you, Laura? What are you looking for?" Hmmm. I had actually pondered this question—without regard to astrology—a few years before Lex and I had physically split but after I'd begun to fear the marital foundation was cracking. I dug up this list from one of my old journals. All these years later, it doesn't seem like this was too much to ask of Lex, though clearly it was.

What I want and *need*:

- to feel appreciated
- to feel respected
- to feel like you are interested in who I am, what I'm doing
- to feel like you're thinking about me
- to have someone who wants to do things with me: *run*, go places, talk, drink and have fun, sleep next to me, and be thoughtful of my feelings

When certified life and relationship coach Amy Schoen was on my podcast, she advised me to determine the qualities I desire in a romantic partner. I decided a short list would be easier to remember when emotions threatened to overrule logic. Let's face it: Sometimes we meet people to whom we're inexplicably drawn. Call it a *spark* or *chemistry*. Maybe even *pheromones*. Whether the chemicals we secret from various body parts actually do subconsciously attract other people is up for scientific debate.[15] But that didn't stop singles in cities including New York, Los Angeles, and Washington, D.C., from holding "pheromone parties." Think speed dating, but instead of people talking to each other, they sniffed previously worn T-shirts to suss out potential partners.[16]

Back to my romantic partner wish list. It is this: smart, active, and funny. *Smart* doesn't singularly mean well educated. It also means having emotional and intellectual maturity and curiosity. It includes Lucy's description of reasonable baggage or, put another way, smart enough to have contained whatever shit has already gone down. *Active* doesn't necessarily mean an Ironman competitor because, geez, people, that's the ability to swim 2.4 miles, cycle for 112 miles, and then run 26.2 miles. Consecutively. On the same day! While I do know some older Reston Runners who regularly compete in similarly hardcore athletic events, I merely want someone who enthusiastically chooses to move and be outside more often than not.

As for *funny*, I define it the way Supreme Court Justice Potter Stewart famously defined porn: I know it when I see it. The dating-site profile that included a photo of a martini next to an open jar of peanut butter with a spoon stuck in it, captioned "Dinner?" I admit, I laughed. The photo of a man wearing a box on his head while holding a huge box-cutter knife . . . not my idea of funny. Also not my idea of funny and, actually, my idea of gross: the close-up photo of a man sticking out his amazingly long, rolled tongue.

Smart, active, and funny. If someone is all three, I can work with whatever else he is. Successful relationships, after all, involve collaboration and compromise. Attraction can grow.

Silly me. I'd forgotten the most important quality of all. It was the gatekeeper quality, the deal-breaker quality. Without it, nothing else mattered.

Regarding astrology, I have anecdotally concluded that many people have an aversion to it for religious reasons. That's why I decided to include here this unaired excerpt of my conversation with astrologer Leslie McGuirk for season 2's "Love in the Stars" podcast episode.

Me: You mentioned God a few minutes ago, and I want to kind of circle back to that because some people might believe that what you're doing is not—you shouldn't be talking about God at all, [that] this is very anti-God. What would you say to that?

Leslie McGuirk: I think astrology is about natural rhythms, natural patterns. And if I was doing fortune-telling, I would agree with them; that is spooky and scary. But if people listen to what I've said, what I'm basically doing is looking with utmost compassion at the way God designed you. And people forget that the magi, the three wise men who found baby Jesus—did you know that *magi* means "astrologer"?

ME: Oh, I didn't know that.

LESLIE: Yeah, it's a huge part of what it means to be wise and what it means to be loving and what it means to be compassionate. I literally call astrology *the language of compassion*. So, we are no different than every other animal on the planet. When you're looking at a basset hound and comparing it to a greyhound, I'm not fortune-telling; I'm telling you that the basset hound has short, stubby legs and a greyhound is much faster and if you put the two of them in a race, the greyhound is going to win. That's what astrology is.

Like, I'm looking at how God created you, how you were designed, and how do we work with the perfection of what you are. It would be very scary if you use astrology in a way that's inappropriate, and that happens a lot. And it's a scary thing, because astrology is a very powerful tool. I spent over twenty years in therapy myself, so I understand a lot about the psychology of what it means to be human. And it's very important, to be believed, that everyone's perfect and that everything's happening just the way it's supposed to.

And sometimes with love, when we aren't getting what we want, sometimes it's because the other person needs to be at such a more elevated level that maybe they're not ready. And you can't be with just anybody if you're looking for something really special.

⟡

LAURA: We were approaching our 20th wedding anniversary, with two marvelous daughters, 5 and 8, when the TV horoscope said of his sign, "You're living an intense love story, but it's time to put things right with your partner." I jokingly said, "Aha!" and then saw his crestfallen face. He broke up with her two months later, and we spent six years trying to rebuild in a terrible tango of taking turns approaching or retreating in mistrust.

Almost twenty years later, I am still alone. He is remarried and has a young son. I cannot remember the last time someone approached me. My gurlfrenz say it's because I refuse to see it. My sister says it's because I won't look anyone in the eye. They all say I am attractive, warm, friendly, interesting. Being bisexual should double my chances, right? But all my friends are all straight women and gay men. Deep fear of being hurt again? Perhaps. —S. Z., Italy

At 77 years of age, I am definitely dating while gray. But I am also doing something else: I am dating while girl, and for me that is a relatively new thing. I was identified as male at birth, and for nearly three-quarters of a century I did what I was supposed to do and tried to date while boy. It did not work.

About forty years ago, I explored the possibility of transition. But the times were different, and I did not. Like many other people, I married the wrong person for the wrong reasons, and that marriage is over. About three years ago, I decided that I did not want to die a boy. I especially did not want to die alone and boy, and [I] finally transitioned. It was absolutely the right thing to do. Dating while girl works. I have had my first relationship, and it was wonderful.

Oops, did I say I am dating while gray? I was dating while gray. Today is the eighth day of my social distancing, and it has been nine days since I have had a hug. Three hugs a day is usually my minimum daily requirement. Five hugs is the normal dose. You may take my word for it: Elbow bumps do not cut it.

Today is the vernal equinox. We get eleven minutes of spring. It is the perfect metaphor for my life. After a lifetime of winter being a boy, I get eleven minutes of the spring as a girl. And I find myself going into isolation knowing that a hug could quite literally kill me. I'm not crying. I'm just numb. —I. H., Maryland.

CHAPTER FIVE

~

Ringers on the Dating Curve

A warm September evening found me in the faux urban-hip Mosaic District, perched at a sidewalk table in front of a tiny Thai café a literal stone's throw from the apartment I called home after splitting with Lex. Across from me sat Sully, a man I'd known since we were kids. Prior to tonight, we hadn't seen or spoken to each other in about forty years. Sully had found my email address and reached out after having a conversation with a random someone with whom, as life would have it, I'd also recently had a conversation.

Sully wrote because he heard I was single. Was I doing okay? He knew it was hard, because he was recently separated. Would I like to get some dinner and catch up? Sure! I said. Why not? Back in the day, Sully had been what we girls called a hunk. (In case you don't know, hunk = hottie.) I remembered him as tall and athletically built, with long, dark-brown hair parted far on one side and framing round blue eyes.

We'd chosen the Mosaic District because it was close to one of Sully's kid's ball fields and close enough to Reston. I recognized him as soon as he arrived: His hair was lighter and shorter, but the browns still outnumbered the grays, and his hairline was fairly robust. He was wearing pleated khakis with a polo shirt that complemented his eyes.

His waist had thickened over the years, but c'mon, whose hadn't? Even with a dad bod, Sully still had it goin' on.

We settled in to peruse the menu and talk. Now, I speak in rough draft even under the most placid of circumstances, but that night I was really stumbling and stuttering. Sully had a way of locking his eyes onto mine as I talked that caused my mouth to shift completely out of gear with my brain.

I told Sully about my recent foray into online dating. I hadn't put much thought into the words or photos I'd posted, yet it had hardly mattered. My lame effort had led to a tsunami of attention from men with tasteless usernames such as Dr. Wood, Mr. Huge, GratKissor (hah, more like lousy speller) and Milfhunter65—M-I-L-F as in, mother I'd like to . . . you know. Then there was Makusqrt12, who told me he was looking for someone honest, hardworking, and freaky. Truly horrified, I'd stopped checking my account even though the three-month trial hadn't expired.

"Online dating makes me feel like a piece of meat that's been thrown into the lion's den." I flirted with Sully in clumsy simile.

"Oh, Laura," Sully leaned over the table, drawing me in with those dreamy peepers as he responded in smooth metaphor. "You *are* a piece of meat that's been thrown into the lion's den."

Sigh. Our magical night lasted three hours before ending with a chaste kiss and plans to get together again the following week or so. And we did, and then we did again the week or so after that, and then again the week or so after that. This went on for a few months: weekday dinners or lunches ending with chaste kisses, occasional texts and emails, and one phone call after Sully had dropped off one of his kids somewhere and had time to kill before making the return trip.

Here's what I learned about Sully: He was smart, with an advanced degree that he'd parlayed into a successful, demanding career where he was considered an expert in his field. He was active; he coached his kids' numerous sports teams and diligently worked off a large weight gain brought on by age and an unhappy marriage. And he was funny, responding to one of my texts asking if he had any interest in meditation with, "Ommmigod, no, I can't sit still that long."

However, I also learned this about Sully: He and his wife of twenty years both had big jobs that led to almost as many problems as possessions. They'd long ago stopped trying to make it work, but they hadn't yet told their kids or other family members, or close couple friends, that they were splitting up. They were sleeping in two different bedrooms on two different floors of their very large home with a very large mortgage. Virginia law allows estranged couples to live under the same roof; Sully and his wife need to be separated for a year before a divorce is final because their kids are younger than eighteen.

But. The divorce clock hadn't started ticking yet. Sully and his wife had no property-settlement agreement. They didn't have any legal-separation plan of any sort in place. Technically, neither one was supposed to be dating. That might explain the private detective that Sully said his wife had hired to follow him.

Also, Sully's conversation with our random mutual connection coincided with my online dating profile popping up as a suggested match for him. Sully wasn't supposed to be dating, but online he was. I never would have found him on my own, because Sully paid extra for a feature called "hidden profile." In other words, he could go browsing online to find women who fit his criteria, but women who went browsing online for men who fit their criteria wouldn't find him. He was in digital hiding—hence, hidden profile. When Sully saw a woman who sparked his interest, he could wink or nod or give a thumbs-up or send a message, inviting her to check out his profile he'd open up temporarily for her eyes only. And wouldn't you know it? Sully wound up winking at one of my best friends.

Smart, active, funny—Sully most certainly was all that. As for, you know, available? Not so much. Sully's separation was an aspiration, a stretch goal. He may have been unhappily married, but he was married. Remember the U.S. population survey? Married people are legally married whether the spouse is present or absent. And "absent" can mean anything from living a continent or state or condo apart, not sleeping in separate bedrooms while plotting the next relationship move. (Legal Caveat One: State divorce laws vary; check with an attorney about dating while legally married, even if separation papers have been filed.) People like Sully, who attempt to get a jump start on a new relationship before officially wrapping up the old one, are ringers on the dating curve. They're messing things up for those of us attempting to separate the gray-dating wheat from the chaff, as it were.

"Yes, but what's the definition of *available*, and how do you know if somebody's available?" asked Jamie, in her late fifties when we first chatted. "Do you say, 'Oh, wait, before we start dating, I want to see your divorce papers'? It's so hard."

Jamie had firsthand knowledge of men with separation aspiration. She'd met Guy at a Meetup event; they'd gone out a few times before Guy admitted that, as Jamie put it, "Things are a little complicated in his life."

Like Sully and his wife, Guy and *his* wife were living unhappily under the same roof in two different bedrooms. Supposedly, his wife also wanted out of the marriage. She, too, was mixing and mingling at Meetup events. Initially, Guy had told Jamie that he was waiting until his youngest child graduated from high school before persuading his wife to work out a property-settlement agreement.

Well, the youngest child graduated a few years ago, and still nothing had changed. Guy's wife may have been mixing and mingling, but according to Guy she'd been dragging her feet on the PSA. Guy consulted a lawyer who'd advised that if Guy left, the wife could make a case for abandonment that would tip any PSA in her favor. Another factor that would benefit the wife PSA-wise: Guy getting laid. (Legal Caveat Two: State divorce laws vary; check with an attorney about the potential repercussions of having sex with someone who's not your legal spouse.)

Jamie was striving to be patient. She believed God had brought Guy into her life to force her to slow down when it came to romantic entanglements. "I'm a believer in long-term relationships," Jamie told me. "And I know that they take a lot of work. And I think it's worth the work if both parties are willing to do it. I just have to trust."

Here's Jamie's history: Her marriage to her college sweetheart, Cal, had ended after three kids and almost twenty years together. The split had been Cal's idea. "I always wanted to be married, always believed in a happily ever after," Jamie said. "I never expected to get divorced. After it happened, I kind of went off the deep end with dating. I fall in love very quickly, which is detrimental to my health."

Jamie had gotten involved with a series of unsuitable men, including an emotionally abusive alcoholic. Finally, after friends intervened on her behalf, Jamie realized she needed to start fresh. So she took her portable, well-paying job in the mid-Atlantic back to her hometown in the Northeast. Very quickly, she met Murray online and then bought a house and invited him to move in with her. Murray arrived with his teenage son and dog. "I thought we were going to have happily ever after," Jamie said. "But it became very difficult."

Jamie discovered she and Murray really didn't have much in common. He liked staying home and resented when she went out with her friends instead of plopping down on the couch alongside him. Then there was the matter of Murray's bragging about having slept with 365 different women the previous year. "He wasn't right for me," Jamie said, "but it took me a while to figure that out. I just went with what my heart felt."

After about a year, they split. "At this point, I'm fifty years old," Jamie told me. "I realized I needed to break the pattern of meeting someone and sleeping with him right away and then staying in the relationship because I desperately wanted it to work out since we'd already slept together."

Jamie quit drinking, revved up her exercise routine, and started seeing a therapist. She decided to move back to the mid-Atlantic, settling into an apartment near her ex-husband's home. Months later, while talking to him about something involving their kids, Cal mentioned he was moving to the West Coast and putting his place on the market. Impulsively, Jamie said she'd be interested in buying it. Oh, and what did Cal think about Jamie asking Cal's mom, Maude, to move in with her?

Wait, did I not mention? Jamie had a complication of her own: Her housemate in her ex-husband's former home was her "outlaw," Maude. It seemed like a sitcom-worthy arrangement, but Jamie said it made sense at the time. Jamie had always gotten along with Maude. Even after divorcing out of the family, Jamie called Maude every birthday and checked in with her occasionally. Maude, who was retired, went through a gray divorce of her own from Cal's father. Two decades later, Maude was still feeling emotionally hurt. Also, she'd been diagnosed with fibromyalgia, an incurable disorder that causes muscle and joint pain as well as extreme fatigue.

"At this point, Maude is living in Georgia," Jamie recounted to me. "She's struggling, and her sons know it, but no one seems to be doing anything about it. I thought if I took Maude in, maybe I could make a difference in her life. I guess I just thought, *This will work out.* And in some respects, it *has* worked out, It's nice living with someone, and it's helpful to share some costs. But in other respects, it hasn't worked out."

Maude couldn't muster the energy to join any support groups or exercise classes that Jamie found for her or to make new friends. She enjoyed sharing meals with Jamie but wasn't as enthusiastic as Jamie was about healthy cooking.

Maude had moved in with Jamie a few days after Jamie closed on Cal's house. A few days after that, Jamie met Guy. Since then, Maude has also met Guy. While they all got along fine, neither Guy nor Jamie felt comfortable hanging out at Jamie's place for extended periods of time. Needless to say, they couldn't hang out at Guy's house. Their dating options clearly were limited. Then again, Guy *was* a married man.

"He's definitely a good guy, but I have a lot of family and friends who are uncomfortable with the situation," Jamie said. She was quick to note that a friend of a friend in the know corroborated Guy's claim that the wife also considered herself separated. "I thought Guy was telling me the truth from the get-go. He doesn't seem like the type who would lie. But Laura, there *are* people who would," Jamie told me. "You hear it all the time, about people who are dating someone they think is single. It happened to a friend of mine recently. She thought she was dating someone who was divorced. But there were a lot of inconsistencies, even with, like, 'Gee, where do you live?' Then she realized he was lying to her."

Jamie said she and Guy had actually met at two separate Meetup events, six months apart. They'd had a wonderful conversation at the first Meetup, but there had been no follow-up, and she'd forgotten about it. Six months later, at the second Meetup, they'd talked again, and he had recounted everything she had told him the first time around. It was after that get-together that Guy had reached out and asked her to dinner.

"He didn't contact me after we met the first time because he didn't consider himself available," Jamie said. "The second time he was available—in his head. But after things started getting more complicated and dragging out, I said to him, 'You know, I really wish that you had waited to date me. Because you really weren't available.'"

By the time Jamie's story aired on the first season of *Dating While Gray*, her outlaw had found a new place to live and her grown child had temporarily moved in. But Guy was still living with his estranged wife, no closer to moving out than he'd been when Jamie first met him. Jamie told me that hearing herself describe her trying situation gave her the courage to break up with Guy. ("Service journalism!" exclaimed Ruth, one of WAMU's podcast producers.) Jamie said she still loved Guy but had decided he needed to figure out next steps on his own, without romantic distractions.

Spoiler alert: The breakup didn't last long. Shortly before the COVID-19 lockdown, they got back together. They see each other whenever they can, and Jamie is back to waiting, more or less patiently, for Guy to be free.

Dear Laura,
Sometimes I feel love is like alcohol. When you are addicted to it, you lose yourself in a world of illusion. Sometimes you can't tell what is right or wrong because your brain is crippled by it. You realize that maybe it won't do you good, but your heart refuses to listen. The power of illusion is unbelievably destructive. Sometimes love does the same. It is sad. —B., China

Hi Laura,
I've been single now longer than I was married, which was 15 years. And much to my surprise, I meet men and it does not work out. There will be some obstacle, like, "Oh yeah, by the way, I should have told you in the beginning I was married." Or some other thing—"I'm a liar, I'm a cheat," whatever. The idea of it being as simple as finding an empty drawer in your bathroom is really funny to me. —N., Maryland

From season 1's "Sage Advice" episode, the following is an excerpt of my interview with writer Sophy Burnham. Now in her mid-eighties, Sophy's body of work is wide and deep. She's also been single for decades, after her

only marriage ended in divorce. I asked her to describe her perspective on dating and relationships.

SOPHY BURNHAM: In spite of being very independent and very much a rebel, I'm also a product of my own culture. And my own culture said, "A woman is not herself sufficient. She must have a man." It's taken me a long time to realize that this is one more of those unnecessary bits of information, like "Opportunity knocks but once," that . . . is completely wrong.

ME: You've been in love. Did you ever come close to living with someone or being in another committed relationship?

SOPHY: I've been in committed relationships, mm-hmm.

ME: It just never got to the point where you wanted to . . . have you ever lived with somebody else?

SOPHY: Well, each one has its own story. One man that I was in love with—deeply in love with, and he with me—was married and separated, and after five years went back to his wife. I certainly expected to marry him. He said to me, "I will marry you, and I want to marry you. I know I'm being difficult." And then two weeks later, he ended up back with his wife because he couldn't stand the pressure of a divorce and what it would do to the family and everything. I understood.

ME: It seems like there are a lot of men out there who are unhappy in their marriage but they don't necessarily want to get divorced.

SOPHY: They can't get out of it.

ME: Right. For whatever reasons.

SOPHY: But dating is hell. Dating is really stupid. So don't look for a date. Don't look for a boyfriend. Find, don't seek. The universe will bring you the right person.

PART II

FINDING

CHAPTER SIX

∼

Perfect (?) Strangers

The following are factual descriptions of men I have met through three different online-dating sites:

- A divorced government official who retired on the early side to spend more time with his special-needs adult child.
- A divorced, high-powered attorney who travels frequently for work. For relaxation, he plays piano and keeps abreast of the restaurant/foodie scene.
- A widowed, late fifties horse farmer who is an audiovisual whiz and metal band aficionado. He enjoys inviting his large circle of friends over for weekend-long campouts with bonfires, sound shows, and craft beer.

On paper, all three fit my list. But for various reasons, none was a love match. Here's what happened with each of them:

I exchanged a few emails with the divorced government official; let's call him Govvy. His communications were grammatically correct and typo-free; his photos were okay. Then, one Saturday morning, he emailed to ask if I'd like to meet him for dinner the following Thursday. Sure, I said. Why not?

"Okay, great," he replied. "Let's get together today for our predate meeting." Now, I know many online dating experts advise a quick meet and greet for a first get-together because there can be a lot of conversation pressure, and expense, to have dinner as your first face-to-face. But I figured Govvy and I had communicated enough by that point, and I wasn't interested in having a predate when I'd already agreed to have a *date*-date. Besides, I had a lot going on that particular day, including getting ready for a ten-mile race very early the next morning.

I tried to get out of it, but Govvy seemed super eager for this predate meeting. Feeling the need to be agreeable, I said, "Okay, I've got an hour this afternoon. Let's meet for tea." So we did and, I have to say, I was pleasantly surprised. Govvy was better looking in person than his photos suggested. We had a good, easy conversation; the hour was over in no time. Afterward, he emailed to say he enjoyed meeting me and good luck with the race.

The next morning, with hopes for my romantic life suddenly high, I ran the ten miles, then went home to soak in the tub and take a long nap. That night, feeling relaxed and also anticipatory, I emailed Govvy to ask where he wanted to meet for dinner on Thursday. Govvy responded quickly to clarify that, yes, he had enjoyed meeting me, but that one hour over tea had opened his eyes to the realization that I wasn't really his type and therefore, there was no point in keeping our dinner date.

Alright, buddy. Your loss.

I went out with the high-powered attorney—let's call him Billable— three times over the course of a couple of months: two dinners and then a concert at Wolf Trap National Park for the Performing Arts. (Great date venue, by the way.) Despite our political differences and slight-stature similarities, I tried hard to ignite within myself some sort of spark for him. I never managed to get a fire going, so to speak. Still, I was puzzled when three or four weeks passed after the concert and I hadn't heard anything from him, not even a response to my text saying I had enjoyed Wolf Trap and was looking forward to seeing him again.

At happy hour one night, I updated my friends on the Billable situation. That's when I learned the term *ghosting*. According to these online-dating wise and weary women, inexplicably withdrawing from all communication is not that uncommon, and it includes blocking one's phone number and online-dating profile. Hearing this, I became not only puzzled but also annoyed—like, who would ever ghost someone else unless personal health and safety concerns required that one break all contact? Perhaps it was the wine that prompted me to pick up my phone and pound out what I thought was a symbolic revenge text. "Yo Lil' Bill," I wrote, "*you* ghosted *me*? Your loss, buddy."

Um, guess what? Billable had *not* blocked my phone number. I learned this uncomfortable fact a few days after sending that text when he responded to it. Oops. Billable said he hadn't even known what ghosting was, had to Google it; apologies for going AWOL, but he'd been super busy with work and travel and had missed my text shortly after the concert and, oh, by the way, he'd really clicked with someone he'd been dating concurrently with me and had decided to become exclusive with her.

Honestly, I didn't have a problem with this.

As for Ozzy, the horse farmer, we met during the COVID-19 lockdown after the first season of my podcast had ended and I'd felt I could get back online without mixing business and pleasure. (To clarify, my feelings about getting back online coincided with my son, Linc, and his fiancée, Julie, surprising me with an online dating account they'd set up for me, using photos from my Facebook page.) My emails with Ozzy quickly progressed to meeting a few times via Zoom. He seemed like he'd be fun to hang out with as a friend, once it was safe to do so. But our lives felt too different to ever merge romantically. He lived ninety miles away, out in the country. His young-adult kids, understandably missing their mom, lived with him with no plans to leave. Plus, once when Ozzy got up to close his window shade to eliminate the glare on his computer screen, I spotted the circular outline of what looked like a chewing tobacco can in his back pocket. Also, metal music? Not a fan.

So, no love connections with any of these three—or, actually, with anyone else I met online. Moreover, for every email exchange, meet and greet, and date I enjoyed or endured, I first had to sift through hundreds, perhaps thousands, of profiles. The MILF hunter. Dr. Wood. The box-wearing and tongue-rolling dudes. Plus:

- A man whose name was Ed and who thought he was special and so went by the username Special Ed

- Mike, who wrote that he desired to become every online dating cliché and thus was casually looking for something serious and wanted a partner in crime to live, laugh, and love with while neither working hard nor playing hard
- Numerous men who attempted to initiate a conversation by merely writing "Hi," "Wassup" or something else equally lacking any effort

Perhaps these men could have been potential romantic partners. Maybe I would have eventually felt a spark had I explored further instead of immediately ignoring, swiping left, or otherwise passing them over. But online dating requires making quick decisions with limited information. Otherwise, it's a huge expenditure of time and energy. Ask anyone, even those who have been successful at finding a partner online, and they'll tell you: Online dating is a lot of work.

"It's foolish to say that it *isn't* work," said renowned biological anthropologist Helen Fisher, when we talked for season 2 of *Dating While Gray*.

"But we're working to find life's greatest prize: a partner," she continued. "You know, we work to keep our health. We work to keep our job. We work to keep our friends."

Helen's a senior research fellow at the Kinsey Institute, where she explores the science behind sexuality, relationships, and well-being. She's also chief scientific advisor to Match.com. As for online dating, "I do think that it is the place to find romance," Helen told me— though her own gray love story involves a journalist whom she met through her work. (More about that in chapter 10.) "Find it anywhere, for God's sake," advised Helen, who's personally a big believer in making and maintaining romantic connections for emotional and even physical well-being. "But if you haven't found it anywhere else," she said, go online.

Anecdotally, it seems to me that a lot of older people have tried online dating at some point. Further, most of us are, indeed, online in that we're accessing dating sites from our laptops or desktop computers instead of using mobile-device dating apps. (I, and the resources cited in this chapter, used the term *online* to include both websites and apps.) But according to a Pew Research Center study conducted in October

2019, only about 16 percent of Americans ages fifty and older have tried online dating: 19 percent of people ages fifty to sixty-four, and 13 percent of those sixty-five-plus.[1] In comparison, the Pew study found that 43 percent of U.S. adults ages eighteen to forty-nine have tried online dating: 48 percent ages eighteen to twenty-nine, and 38 percent in the thirty to forty-nine age bracket. Keep in mind, though, that the Pew study didn't specifically focus on uncoupled older people or on people who coupled up after the age of fifty. Those lines of inquiry may have uncovered different results.

Still, the Pew study found that a lot of older people considered online dating risky behavior—and remember, this study was conducted before the pandemic. About 55 percent of people ages fifty and older called online dating "not at all safe" or "not too safe" compared with 39 percent of those ages thirty to forty-nine.

More distressing news about online dating comes from Nancy Jo Sales's book *Nothing Personal: My Secret Life in the Dating App Inferno*. A journalist, best-selling author, and documentary filmmaker in her late fifties, Nancy Jo was an early user of online dating sites when she was in her thirties and divorced. Then, she turned to dating apps a few months before she turned fifty, after another supposedly forever relationship had ended. She met many men and had a lot of sex, good and bad; at one point, she thought she was in love. But her personal experiences, as well as taking a deep dive into research, led Nancy Jo to ultimately conclude that dating apps promote hookup culture and are more focused on collecting data from their millions of users and keeping them "in the game," so to speak, than in fostering long-lasting love connections.[2]

I desperately hope Nancy Jo's experiences were skewed. She used dating apps, which seem to me to encourage making swift decisions based on photos alone. Would she have found a lasting connection had she thoughtfully perused profiles via a laptop or desktop computer or if she had focused on nonmillennial men?

Also, Nancy Jo's online-dating experiences had occurred before COVID-19 became a dreaded reality. Some people have been hopeful that the pandemic would usher in a kinder, gentler era for online dating that will stick around long after social distancing is a thing of the past. In early June 2020, about three months into the U.S. shutdown, the *New York Times* asked over five hundred epidemiologists to predict when it would be safe to resume everyday activities such as meeting new people, aka dating. While 2 percent actually said never (who are these cruel people?) the majority, 42 percent, said it would be a year or more. The next-highest percentages, each at 16 percent, believed it would be safe by fall 2020 or spring 2021.[3]

The rollout of the COVID-19 vaccines proved to be a social game changer. By mid-November 2021, 86 percent of Americans ages sixty-five and older were fully vaccinated against COVID-19.[4] Fully vaccinated people were able to safely gather indoors or outdoors with other fully vaccinated people without wearing masks or staying socially distanced, leading some online daters to include their vaccine status in their profile. In fact, the White House COVID-19 response team announced in May 2021 that Tinder, Bumble, Hinge, Plenty of Fish, and other dating sites were offering special deals for users who got vaccinated. (Presumably this was to encourage the under-fifty daters, who are statistically more vaccine reluctant.)[5]

Older people in particular might not have wanted to wait too long for a face-to-face; to put it starkly while also contradicting the Rolling Stones, time is *not* on our side. But lightning-speed physical connections seem so pre-2020. Instead, many people began practicing what the Bumble blog calls "slow dating": spending more time getting to know each other through emails, phone calls, and video chats before cautiously progressing to in-person meetings.[6] Ozzy and I figured out Zoom on our own, but some dating sites added video features. Match.com, for example, introduced Vibe Check during the pandemic. After members match, one can quickly invite the other to a live video conversation.[7]

"If you're single and you want to be in a relationship, you don't want to put it on hold too much," relationship and life coach Greg Wheeler told me during the height of the pandemic, before the COVID-19 vaccines had rolled out. Formerly an engineer, Greg had switched careers in 2016 after going through his own divorce and raising four kids. He now helps people gently break romantic connections and also make new ones.

Greg recommends using an online-dating service with video calling—and to get to the video part as quickly as possible. "In a pandemic, we're forced to spend more time communicating," he noted. "So you can get to know someone better before meeting. You can call them, you can take them on a walk with you and your phone, and get to be friends." The video aspect, he added, eliminates any concerns that someone might be misrepresenting their true identity.

Dating app Filter Off launched in February 2020. Users sign up for a "date night" based on their location or interests and then are set up with at least three prospects. You get ninety seconds to connect live on video; afterward, you decide whether to continue with a virtual relationship or move on.[8] The company's PR rep, Michelle, told me that the baby boom generation comprises 8 percent of all users. "They're turning to Filter Off because they're looking for an app that doesn't require much time and provides an authentic dating experience," she said.

Back to the Pew study. It finds that, overall, people believe online dating is a legit way to meet romantic partners. Half of those surveyed ages fifty and older felt a relationship that started online could be as successful and long-lasting as a relationship that began by meeting organically. Problem is, few of the surveyed had personally experienced online dating success. Only 12 percent had married or entered into a committed relationship with someone they first met online. Additionally, 23 percent said they'd never scored even a single date with someone through online dating. This could be why people were feeling more frustrated (45 percent) than hopeful (28 percent) about online dating.[9]

How, then, can we explain the findings of Michael J. Rosenfeld? The Stanford University sociology professor has conducted research into how people find romantic partners. The paper that caught my attention was titled, "Marriage, Choice, and Couplehood in the Age of the Internet."[10]

Though I spent almost forty minutes interviewing Michael for season 1 of *Dating While Gray*, I wound up using only a twenty-second sound bite. The professor and I didn't exactly have what one might call "audio chemistry." Not that I doubted the scientific validity of his work. I just, you know, had a really hard time believing it. Michael has been married for more than thirty years to his college sweetheart. He has never, ever ventured online for personal reasons. Seems to me it's like getting romantic relationship advice from a Catholic priest. Or perhaps it's like a general deciding on battle strategy from his cushy Pentagon office instead of getting input from boots on the ground. I'll let you decide, based on an unaired excerpt of our interview:

MICHAEL ROSENFELD: We looked at a nationally representative sample of American adults and asked them how they'd met their partners. And of course, in recent years, meeting online has become more and more popular. And it has, in fact, displaced all the other ways of meeting . . . through friends, through family, at work, at church, in secondary school, and every other way.

ME: Wow. And I'm assuming that before the Internet, these were the ways, the primary ways, that people met. But are you saying now [the] Internet is number one, hands down, across all ages?

MICHAEL: Internet is the number one way couples meet now, for people of all ages and for heterosexual couples and same-sex couples.

ME: Wow. So these findings were regardless of age. But if you look at just people fifty and older, was the statistic more pronounced?

MICHAEL: It's similar, maybe even a little more pronounced, because a lot of people fifty and older are no longer in the workplace, right? If you're [in your] seventies or eighties, you're not in the workplace. It's harder to meet somebody at work if you're not working. If you're eighteen years old and living with your parents, it's a lot easier for your parents to set you up with somebody or introduce you to somebody than if you're seventy years old and your parents are deceased. So some of the traditional ways of meeting don't work for older people.

[Rosenfeld then noted that older women outnumber their male counterparts, so heterosexual women are in what he calls a *thin dating market.*] That means the advantage of the Internet is really powerful for them, because one of the things that the Internet can provide is wider choice set. Wider choice set is advantageous for everyone who's in a thin dating market.

The ratio of frogs to princes has always been high. And if you want to meet somebody great, you might have to go through quite a lot of bad dates. And the advantage of the Internet is that it's possible to go through more of the bad dates and to meet more people. And that raises your chances of meeting the one person or the two people you think are really terrific who are also going to think that you're terrific. It's not an easy thing to accomplish. And so the more people you have access to, the better your chances are.

Me: Anyone who's ever ventured online knows it can be very overwhelming. The minute you put up your picture and your profile, you're swamped with hundreds of responses. And then if you want to, you can go out and, literally, look for somebody to date anywhere in the world. And it reminds me of a [different] study . . . that too many options can paralyze someone from making a decision or from feeling satisfied with the decision they made.

Michael: Yeah, this is the famous theory of choice overload. I don't think choice overload applies to dating.

Me: So you have never personally done an app or online dating?

Michael: Never. Sometimes I have to ask my graduate students to explain it to me.

So is online dating a big flop for older people, as the Pew research suggests? Or, as Michael insists, is it the key to finding a partner? One thing the professor and I do agree on: Sifting through the choice set is a lot of work. That's why along with the boom in online-dating sites has come a boom in coaches to help ensure we are set up to succeed with the technology. Coaches offer tips on topics including profile writing and photo composition. (Did you know, for example, that heterosexual women reportedly consider men less dateable if their online profile includes a photo of them holding a cat?[11])

Bela "the Love Guru" Gandhi is a longtime coach in the love business. Based in Chicago, she runs what she calls a dating academy. Bela also has made a career out of being the go-to expert for dating segments on national television programs such as Good Morning America and The Steve Harvey Show. With the onset of the COVID-19 pandemic, she shifted from in-person consultations to remote hour-long online sessions ($250 to $400 per session) and to longer, even pricier webinars.[12] A few years before the pandemic, I paid thirty-five dollars to attend Bela's ninety-minute live webinar, Dating After Fifty. She told us about a hundred people were on the call that one night alone.

The striking and longtime married Bela proved to be part aggressively cheerful teacher, part manic coach. She told us we must be "psychotic optimists" about coupling up. Love will come to us. Not if, but when. However, we must not sit around passively waiting for love to come to us. We must "date like heck" until we find it. But we can't let anyone see us sweat. "We're going to go easy, breezy, macaroni cheesy," Bela told us. (Yes, she really did say that.)[13]

During the seminar and afterward, in her free e-book *The 4 Commandments of Online Dating Success*, Bela offered what I thought were helpful tips on writing effective online profiles, snapping results-guaranteed photos, and contacting potential matches. She suggested we follow a routine: Choose potential dates, email back and forth a few times, and then talk on the phone before proceeding to a face-to-face meeting. She suggests there may be fewer available men than women because men are more process-oriented. They quickly learn and follow the rules for "playing the online dating game," Bela says, and thus they find partners quickly. They go for volume, she says. We all should go for volume.

Honestly, this session with Bela left me feeling weary. It's the same way I felt after my one and only date with Jim, whom I'd met online. After we strolled through the National Portrait Gallery and then walked to a nearby bar for some wine, Jim spent the rest of the evening explaining to me his "numbers guy" approach to online dating.

Jim had set up a series of searches with key attributes. He regularly searched and sorted and tinkered so that the dating-site algorithm frequently updated the list of possible matches he was sent. Jim dated regularly; he even had a couple of months-long relationships. He kept an online dating calendar and meticulously recorded notes to jog his memory in case the volume became overwhelming.

Months after we went out, Jim met another woman who happened to be named Laura and who happened to live in Reston. After about three years of dating, they moved in together. They'd been a couple for well over four years when, in June 2021, they got dressed up, grabbed some flowers, and tied the knot at the county courthouse.

Jim and I weren't a match, but he was a good sport. When I contacted him to ask for an interview for season 1 of the podcast, he agreed. "I remembered you without looking you up in my online calendar," he said. "But I did look up my calendar entry, and here's your Match summary about yourself: 'In the garden of life, I'm more the gardener type than the flower type.'" Yes, amused people, that was my go-to line in my early online-dating days.

Jim and I met for the podcast interview in the food court of a popular grocery store. After he repeated for tape his strategic approach to online dating, I sighed. I wanted to believe, I said, that finding the One isn't strategy but magic.

"I think it's both," replied Jim, noting that while he was being very strategic about finding potential partners, Laura was the one who'd reached out first.

"I really look at it as both," Jim repeated. "I mean, every date is a potential magical opportunity."

From season 1's "The Pursuit of Love" episode, the following is an excerpt of my chat with Robin and Girard, at times playfully bickering as they told the story of how they met through online dating. Each had been married and divorced once; it took them ten years to find each other! They got married in 2019.

GIRARD: What attracted me to women when I was in my twenties and thirties and forties are not the same things now. I need to know about your spiritual connection. And I don't need someone who reads the Bible every day but someone who at least has a firm belief in a higher power. That can be Buddha—whatever it is, as long as you believe in it and you have a spiritual connection with this universe that we live in.

ROBIN: You would think—at least my friends think—I would meet people in the profession that I'm in. And I have met some, but they just didn't stick. So I decided to go online. And I dated a couple of people, but we weren't on the same page. We had some things in common, but the things that were important to me didn't seem to be important to them.

I looked at [Girard's online dating profile] page a couple of times. I really dove into his profile, and I'm like, *Is this guy for real?* One thing, he's really into fitness; I mean mind, body, soul. Close to his mom—okay, that's a biggie, because it shows how he's going to treat you.

He had, "This is what I'm looking for. This is what I'm about. And if you're interested, then hit me up." So I wondered, is he really for real? I said, "Okay. Let me hit him up." We went back and forth online maybe three or four times. And then we actually exchanged telephone numbers.

GIRARD: Yes.

ROBIN: And we talked, and we decided we would meet. So we said, "Okay, let's meet somewhere informal, where we can go and just maybe have a soft drink or whatever." And this way if we had no connection, no hard feelings. He's not paying for a meal.

GIRARD: We went to Panera.

ROBIN: Panera. I was there first, and I waited fifteen minutes. He was late.

GIRARD: I went to the wrong part of Tysons [Corner Center].

ROBIN: Okay, but you were the one who said that it's this Panera.

GIRARD: I was wrong about where it was.

ROBIN: And I thought, you picked it so you knew where it was.

GIRARD: I thought I knew. [Laughter]

ROBIN: When he walked in, I immediately knew it was him because he looked like his [dating profile] photos. I was like, *Okay, he's attractive. You know, he's late but, yeah, he's attractive.* [Laughter]

GIRARD: She looked like her pictures, which was great. So I could tell by her body that she probably ran track in college or high school because the way she was built up. She had on a dress.

ROBIN: Because it was in the summertime.

GIRARD: It was summertime.

ROBIN: It was like July or . . .

GIRARD: It was summertime. And we got to talking. And I knew there was a possibility of a relationship because one, on this particular day, the air conditioning in that part of the Tysons mall was dead. And we stayed and talked to each other for about two hours. That let me know, okay, there was a natural rhythm, a natural want to be around each other.

And then when she [got up to use the restroom], I looked at her [body and] said *Okay, cool.* [Laughter] And she came back, and we were talking and talking and talking about various things. She seemed really nice. And I said, *Okay, I like her.*

Robin: Thanksgiving, we went down to my brother's house in North Carolina, and [Girard] was doing the turkey like we had been together for years!

Girard: Well, around this time I was dating other people too.

Robin: See, I didn't know that.

Girard: Well, you didn't need to know that [because] I chose you. [Laughter]
Everyone that I met who knew her always talked about how great a person she was. Her style of dress—I like to dress. I needed someone who liked to dress. And then she likes to dance, and I like to dance. We had a lot of good things in common.

Robin: When you're used to being the breadwinner who's taking care of everything as a single parent, you're just used to doing things and having control, that sort of thing. He's very, very dominant, very alpha male. And so it took a moment. But I think we've worked through that, and we talked through it. And every now and then, he will bring things to my attention—to stop acting like his mom. And so that was something we talked about. And I recognize that because that's just how I am with my brothers.

Girard: Yeah, but there's certain places where you should be my mom, I want you to be my mom. Like when I'm sick. Okay? [Laughter]

In 20 years of being single, I have tried many dating sites . . . still single but have learned about myself with every meetup. I also learned how to keep myself safe, how to recognize old photos [and] scam setups, and decided I would say "no thank you" rather than ghost. We can all be kind in whatever milieu we are in. —R. G. A.

Although I met several women from [online dating sites] few turned out to be as represented. Most . . . lied about their ages and weights, some significantly. For me, using Internet dating sites was pretty much a waste of time. Although during this pandemic it may be nearly impossible to do so, I have found getting off the couch and out into the world is the best way to meet prospective dates and mates. When I went to Trader Joe's a few days ago, it felt like the very friendly masked lady cashier was checking me out along with my groceries. —B. W.

Men online lie about their age, weight, height, and vitality. They also lie about their marital or relationship status. If you meet a man online who can't date you on weekends and/or wants to meet in towns away from where you both live and/or wants to get physical real fast, *beware*. —L. B.

I've been ghosted, insulted, stood up, and asked for a booty call all while trying multiple online dating sites at different times. I don't embellish my profile or lie about weight, height, etc. I'm a straight shooter. In my personal experience, it's been a waste of time and money, although I have several friends who have successful long-term relationships that started online. —G. Y.

Laura,

I'm 70 and recently met someone online. We decided not to wait for a face-to-face. Socially distanced dating is not really a new concept. Recall the scene in *The Godfather* when Michael meets and courts Apollonia while on the lam in Sicily. On their first date, they stroll the local hills, walking only close enough to hold a conversation.

My date was like that, except we weren't shadowed by a contingent of armed chaperones. We met in a parking lot, fully masked, for a stroll along a trail. As we walked, we encountered others and, like two magnets with the same poles facing, we gracefully kept a buffer as we passed. At length, we were able to find a place away from other people where we could sit, remove our masks, and talk at a distance. We both had our cameras, so we took photos of each other.

There was no cortado with our knees pressed together under a small table in the shade of a tree; no glass of Rhône blend, shoulder to shoulder, at La Jambe; no standing in awe before a John Singer Sargent at the National Gallery of Art; no searching for rapini at the farmer's market; no Art Hop in Takoma Park; no gently touching her forearm to get her attention; no holding hands; no hugging when it concluded. No need to rush things. —S. H.

Met my BF online three and a half years ago at 55. Still together. Sometimes it works!

Dear Laura,
I am 61, married 23 years, divorced now for nearly twelve. I feel like I've been giving it an honest effort, but the pickins are slim here in the happiest city in America, San Luis Obispo. I will say I have met a lot of nice men, good men, on the dating sites, but few that have left me wanting more. In the past eight years, I have probably gone out with nearly 100 men, but only a handful for a second or third date and even less would I call a relationship. I keep thinking, is it me? What am I doing wrong? But, honestly, if I can't think of anything else I'd like to talk to him about, that's a sure sign it isn't going to work. And I don't want to waste anyone's time. I think I have a lot to offer the right person, but I want to be with someone who will lift me up, bring something interesting to the table. I don't want to settle just so I won't be alone. Haven't had sex for nearly five years now. :(I am not ready to give up, but boy is it discouraging. —K .P.

Hi there! My first husband died in 2006. A year later I went online and within a few days met my (now) second husband. We are very happy together. I was also very happy with my first husband whom I married in my early 40s. So I have had statistics against me every step of the way! —T. A.

Hi Laura!
I'm a widow and have been doing the online dating thing on and off, in short bursts, for the last three years. I have gone on about 30 "coffees" (I *always* pay) and had an attempt at a relationship with one man last year. He was lovely, kind, gorgeous, my age (57), but he had had some kind of traumatic childhood and would not talk about his past at all. In fact, he got angry when I asked. It was in this way I learned all about emotionally unavailable men.

I stopped online dating because it was just SO much work and they all lie and/or have ulterior motives. I'm a spiritual person, and I believe in miracles. We're on [COVID-19] lockdown anyway. If the universe wants to send me a man, then a man will show up when the time is right, and he'll be the man I want. Not a "good enough" man, but the perfect match. —V. C., Virginia

A friend told me his worst experience of someone not being honest on their profile was when his date neglected to share that she was in her third trimester of pregnancy. Why in the world would someone not disclose that?? —B. N.

Hello Laura!
I am 56 and have been single for a while. I recently got online for the first time ever because you gave me the boost of confidence I needed. Bless you and thank you!! —G. G. T.

Hi Laura! I am 56, divorced after a 23-year relationship, and now very happily remarried to a divorcé. He was in the online-dating scene for years and was nearly ready to give up when we found one another, despite an algorithm that matched us only 70 percent. —J. D.

To: Laurta Stassi
Subject line: LAST CHANCE! Laurta!

Hi Laurta! I AM SO EXCITED FOR YOU!! Why? Because you're gonna turn into a positive, psychotically optimistic dating rockstar at our webinar TONIGHT! . . .

PS: Laurta, love is not going to come down your chimney. Take action and do SOMETHING.
PPS: . . . The Love Lab (only 1 SPOT LEFT) . . . will most likely be closed tonight (and there's a $503 discount right now.) You are going to kick yourself if you don't do this. Laurta Stassi you keep looking at it—just do it! Love you! Bela

~

CHAPTER SEVEN

Friend of a Friend

Stefan was in his fifties when he finally realized that staying unhappily married to his equally unhappy wife for the sake of their two teenagers was actually having a negative impact on the kids' well-being. So he moved out of the family home shortly before they graduated from high school, settling into a place close by. When the financial and emotional dust had settled and Stefan was officially divorced, he started looking for a new romantic partner. He joined an online dating site.

As part of the registration process, Stefan was asked to describe his own body type and also to indicate which body type he preferred for potential romantic partners. Stefan enjoyed running, cycling, hiking, swimming—in fact, an active lifestyle was one thing he and his ex-wife had in common. So he accurately described himself as "athletic/fit." For his preferred body type, perhaps with his ex in mind, he chose two: "slim/slender" and "athletic/fit."

Christine had been a stay-at-home mother of four young children when her husband's infidelities led to divorce. She relocated, found a full-time job, and started working on a graduate degree to improve her career opportunities. About five years postdivorce, Christine was finally able to eke out some time for herself. She bought a bicycle and started cycling to work a few days a week. On the rare weekend she wasn't traveling for her graduate program and the kids were with their dad, she asked a friend to join her for a leisurely hike. Sometimes she ran with work colleagues during the lunch hour.

Christine also joined an online dating site—the same one, in fact, that Stefan was on. When asked to pick her preferred body type for potential romantic partners, Christine indicated "no preference." But when asked to describe her own body type, she hesitated. "Slim/slender" and "athletic/fit" seemed too small. "Muscular," "big and beautiful," and "heavyset" seemed too large. "A few extra pounds" seemed defeat-ist; "about average" seemed like a cop-out. So Christine settled on what she considered to be the most accurate, and positive, descriptor: "curvy."

Stefan and Christine met; they clicked from the get-go. Coinciden-tally, they lived only a few miles apart. They also had similar values and goals. Stefan was attracted to Christine's ambition and exuberance, not to mention her curvy body. Christine, in turn, appreciated Stefan's entrepreneurial drive, sense of adventure, and kind and generous spirit toward her kids. They dated steadily for about a year before becom-ing engaged: romantic dinners and getaways, plus hiking and cycling adventures included both sets of kids. In 2021, Stefan and Christine celebrated their twelfth wedding anniversary.

Another online-dating success story? Not even close. Despite being on the same dating site at the same time and living in practically the same neighborhood, the site's algorithm failed to suggest Stefan as a match for Christine, or Christine as a match for Stefan. Instead, they got together thanks to a couple named Bodhi and Jerrie. Bodhi and Stefan had worked in the same industry for years; Jerrie and Christine's friendship began in college.

Here's how the setup happened: Bodhi and Jerrie, both extroverts, were in the telecommunications industry. They started a networking group and hosted multiple get-togethers. One of the biggest was a summer party that reliably drew a crowd of more than two hundred people. The summer party was where Stefan and Christine met. Stefan was there as a member of the networking group. Christine was there because Jerrie invited her.

Jerrie told me that introducing Stefan and Christine wasn't neces-sarily premeditated. But the moment during the crowded party when she was talking to Christine and glanced over to see Bodhi talking to

Stefan, a light bulb went off. "Bodhi and I are networkers; we're connectors," Jerrie explained. "It's in our DNA. Whenever we have single friends, it's a thought that simmers in our minds: *Who can we introduce them to?*"

Friend of a friend: it's a longtime tried-and-true method for finding a romantic partner. Perhaps it's more effective than online dating, considering algorithms such as the one that failed to match Stefan and Christine. Then again, maybe we can't place all the blame on the algorithm. It was Stefan, after all, who directed the site to avoid sending him profiles of anything but slim/slender and athletic/fit women. No slam on Stefan; based on his life experiences, he couldn't envision that a woman who enjoyed the activities he enjoyed might be built any other way.

So it's possible none of us really knows for certain what we want in a romantic partner. "It's really easy to spend time hunting around online for someone who seems to match your ideals," says behavioral scientist Jehan Sparks. "But our research suggests an alternative approach."[1]

Jehan was a doctoral student at the University of California–Davis when a study she led was published in the *Journal of Experimental Social Psychology*. The study found that people are attracted to those who fit the top three qualities they desire in a romantic partner. However, people also are attracted to those who fit the top three qualities that *others* desire in a romantic partner. For example, let's say you're looking for someone who is thoughtful, kind, and inquisitive. In case you forgot from chapter 4, I've been looking for someone smart, active, and funny. According to Jehan's study, you'd be as likely to be attracted to someone who is thoughtful, kind, and inquisitive—your wish list—as you would be to someone who is smart, active, and funny—my wish list. Therefore, you didn't have special insight into what you actually want in a romantic partner; hence, the study's name: "Negligible Evidence that People Desire Partners Who Uniquely Fit Their Ideals."[2] As Jehan says, "Don't be too picky ahead of time about whether a partner matches your ideals on paper. Or, even better, let your friends pick your dates for you."[3]

I've certainly been game. If you've been reading this book closely, you'll recall I've utilized this method. Remember twice-widowed Mark, from chapter 4? I was introduced to him via email by Shevaun, a longtime friend of mine from Richmond. Mark and his first wife, Nancy, were together almost thirty-five years. She'd been diagnosed with multiple sclerosis early in the marriage, but it wasn't until the last few years of her life that the disease progressed to the point she needed a caregiver. Mark expected he would outlive Nancy, but he was stunned when she died two weeks after a simple bladder infection led to a downward spiral.

Unexpectedly, Mark found new love fairly quickly when he reconnected with a former coworker named Jeanette. They became serious within months after Nancy's death, then got married less than a year after that. Days after they returned home from their honeymoon, Jeanette was diagnosed with lung cancer. She died sixteen months later.

Mark had been on his own for a few years by the time he and I met. Shevaun vaguely remembered Mark from working with him a few years before he'd retired. One of her coworkers had more recent, fond memories. The recommendation came with some dust on it, but I loved Shevaun. And I knew she had great taste in men because her longtime husband, Richard, is a gem.

Mark wasn't active on social media, so before we met I didn't know what he looked like or who and what his other connections and interests were. In fact, other than the twice-widowed part, I really didn't know anything about him before agreeing to a Friday-night date. He had traveled to Northern Virginia from Richmond to supervise renovations on the condo he'd recently purchased to live close to his grown kids and grandchildren.

On that first date, I learned Mark was a really nice guy as well as another eventual good sport who agreed to be interviewed for the *Dating While Gray* podcast. He was featured in the season 1 episode called "The Pursuit of Love." But I also learned Mark was looking for a traveling companion, and I was nowhere near retiring. Also, he seemed very eager for me to meet his family at a cookout planned for the Sunday after our date. Not that I'm all that, but I didn't want to get everyone's hopes up that I was going to be a keeper, especially because of the twice-widowed thing. I'm sorry, it did give me pause.

My second friend-of-a-friend connection was Gary, whom I met through my running buddy Kurt. Here's where I tell you that, despite our disappointing first date, which I covered in chapter 4, I went out with Gary (he of monkey flame) a few more times after that. I really wanted to like Gary because, as you may remember from chapter 3, I really liked Kurt. But Gary and I didn't have anything in common other than that we both were single and we both thought highly of Kurt. Gary and I didn't share the same ideas about politics, religion, or how and when to spend money. We didn't even have parental status in common, as he was childless.

So two friend-of-friend strikes for me, but I appreciated the attempts. And I'm always open to trying again. In fact, after I talked with Jerrie and Bodhi about their role in getting Stefan and Christine together, Jerrie emailed me. "I'm thinking Bodhi and I need to put our 'connecting-the-dots' skills to work for you as well," she wrote. "Who knows what might turn up?" To which I replied, "Please! I'm totally open to dot-connecting!"

According to certified life and relationship coach Amy Schoen, "connectors" like Bodhi and Jerrie are exactly who to tap to utilize the friend-of-a-friend dating strategy. "There are people who have networks of people," Amy told me during our interview for the "Flying Solo" podcast episode. "They love connecting people."

Amy suggested seeking out these connectors, and "then you give them something to remember about you." That "something" is like a thirty-second infomercial or elevator speech describing five to seven things about you: Who you are, what you value, what you're looking for. Once you figure that out, Amy suggested writing it down and adding it to the notes app on your mobile phone. That way, you could easily refer to it when talking with connectors. The connectors, in turn, would then be able to efficiently search their inventory of people for potential matches.

Here's another confession: I've done a little friend-of-a-friend connecting myself. For better or for worse, though, I wasn't strategic. Perhaps I was inspired by remembering that back in the nineties, actress Jennifer Aniston had briefly dated Counting Crows lead singer Adam Duritz before introducing him to her *Friends* costar and real-life bestie Courteney Cox, who also went on to date him briefly.[4] In other words, as long as I could vouch for basic good character while being transparent about my lack of insight into whether two people actually would click, what was the harm in sending them on a potentially bad date or leading them to a relationship that didn't work out?

Thus, a couple of months after "The Pursuit of Love" aired, I asked Poncie, then WAMU's senior podcast producer, her thoughts on the following email I received:

Hello Laura,
I've been listening to your podcast and think it's great for people like us. I'm 59, have been single for four years, and think online dating is a freak show. You recently interviewed a man named Mark . . . whom you mentioned that you dated once. I've listened to that segment twice, and I liked all of his answers. The question is: Is it against your policy to connect people through a situation like this? "If you don't ask, the answer is always no!" Looking forward to your answer . . .

Poncie assured me I wouldn't be violating any public radio podcast journalism standards. So I forwarded the email to Mark with the caveat I knew nothing about this person, not even where she lived. Mark told me later that he reached out—the woman *was* local—but it went nowhere fast.

"We exchanged two very general introductory emails, then she wanted to exchange photos," Mark told me. "After I sent her mine, she replied that the ten-year age difference between us is too much and that she needs to stick with someone her age or younger."

So a swing and a miss and, also, ouch. "Don't feel bad," Mark told me. "My feelings aren't hurt. She was honest and pleasant about it. *C'est la vie.* There's always a next time."

There *was.* With Mark's permission, I gave his email address to Evamarie, whose story also was featured in "The Pursuit of Love." If you heard the episode, you know all about Evamarie. Now in her late fifties, she grew up in a small town in Pennsylvania and had always assumed she'd get married one day. She hadn't. After graduating from college, she started her journalism career in the D.C. area, where she lived almost twenty-four years. After job setbacks and the death of her mom, Evamarie moved back to Pennsylvania to take care of her dad. He died six months later, and Evamarie struggled financially, emotionally, and physically. Slowly, she regained equilibrium.

"I remember a friend of mine asking me, 'What would it take to get you to come back here [to D.C.]?'" Evamarie told me. "And I said, the job of a lifetime. That or love."

It wasn't love that brought her back to the area, but return she did. After settling into the rhythms of the dream job she'd landed, Evamarie started thinking about an old boyfriend from her late twenties. "We had been Facebook friends at one point, and then all of a sudden he just kind of disappeared," she said. "And I didn't know what had happened. So just in a sentimental mood, I Googled him—and found his obituary."

Learning of his death hit Evamarie hard. "I just remember thinking . . . *We're not getting any younger*. And I [said] to myself, *What are you doing? You want to be in a relationship, but you're not trying*."

So Evamarie decided to go online. She joined a dating site and in the first week had four dates lined up. "I told my friends, you might want to play the lottery because . . . there's been a disturbance in the force," Evamarie said, laughing.

She also exchanged emails and texts with other romantic candidates. For reasons including being immediately queried for "intercourse," getting ghosted, and discovering the existence of presumably clueless wives, Evamarie did not find a lasting romantic connection. She told me during the podcast that while she was happy—she had a great job and a strong circle of supportive friends—she'd love to have a romantic partner in her life.

"Including my deceased former boyfriend, I guess I can say that there have been three great loves of my life," she said. And with all three, "I felt like I was understood, and I felt like I was known, and I felt like I knew somebody. Love makes you an outrageous optimist. You think everything is possible, and you think that everyone should find this and have this. . . . And if, for whatever reason, it doesn't work out, it . . . can be devastating."

Evamarie continued: "You know that old saying, it's better to have loved and lost then never to have loved at all? It's like, yeah, but ultimately, it's better to have loved and kept."

In my interview with Mark on that same episode, he shared his own struggles with online dating since the death of his second wife. "I have spent huge amounts of money on, you know, dinners and lunches. I've been ghosted so much, I feel like Casper," he told me. "One woman said that she just didn't like the way I drove and . . . couldn't see sitting in the car with me for any long distance."

Later, Mark wrote me an email, which he gave me permission to read aloud for the show. "When I was young, life was fully ahead of me," he'd written. "If a relationship didn't work out, no big deal. There were plenty of other women, and I had all the time in the world to find the right one. As time and failed relationships go by, I find myself thinking that meeting someone with whom I can have a serious, committed relationship isn't going to happen. And that is discouraging. I haven't given up hope. I'm just finding it more and more difficult."

The episode with Mark's and Evamarie's interview was released in mid-March 2020, just as WAMU joined other workplaces as well as schools, retail establishments, and other public spaces the world over in shutting down to prevent the spread of COVID-19. A few weeks later, I received a listener email saying she'd been touched by both Mark's and Evamarie's stories. "Maybe you should matchmake some of the people sharing on your podcast," she wrote. "Just an idea; I am ever the hopeful one."

I contacted Evamarie. Would she want to meet Mark? "Huh! Interesting question. I found Mark's story compelling," she replied. "Let me think about that one!" A few days later, Evamarie wrote to say she'd listened to Mark's story again and, yes, she'd be interested in getting in touch. "Can't really go out with anyone anywhere right now, but maybe he'd appreciate chatting," she said. "I know I would."

So then I broached the topic with Mark: okay if Evamarie reached out to him? He said yes; I gave Mark's email address to Evamarie and then stepped out of the way. Evamarie reported later that they'd emailed back and forth a few times before progressing to long phone calls, video chats and, finally, in-person outdoor meetings a safe distance apart before they received COVID-19 vaccines. A growing friendship that filled an aching social void during the pandemic or something more? If you missed the season 2 podcast episode with the Evamarie-Mark update, you'll have to wait until the epilogue of this book to find out.

Sometimes friend-of-a-friend connections happen by accident. Francine was the first person I ever interviewed for the *Dating While Gray* blog, long before my writing project morphed into a podcast.

Francine had filled many roles in her almost seven decades of life, including stay-at-home mom, schoolteacher, part owner of a family business, and now, real estate attorney in Nashville with her own practice. But after getting divorced for a third time shortly before she turned fifty, Francine vowed the one role she would never play again is "wife."

As for marriage, "I just was done," Francine told me with a laugh. She was laughing because she's energetic and fun-loving, and laughing comes easily for her. She also was laughing because about fifteen years after making that promise, Francine had walked down the aisle for a fourth time. Never say never.

Meet Jack, a retired grocery store executive about a decade younger than Francine. The story of how they met seemed so happenstance that romantics could only conclude it was meant to be. They were introduced to each other on the 2013 Fourth of July weekend in Panama City, Florida. Francine owned a condo there. So did the Professor, Jack's childhood best friend from their Alabama hometown. Francine and the Professor knew each other from the online dating site Plenty of Fish.

"Francine is very open, vivacious, and easy to talk to," the Professor told me. They'd met in 2012 and "hit it off very quickly. But we also knew very quickly that this wasn't going to be a romance. We even said to each other that there must be a reason we were brought together, that we were supposed to meet. And we said this to each other somehow knowing we were supposed to be just friends. And that was good."

So while Francine and the Professor were never romantically entwined, they enjoyed each other's company and over the next year got together for drinks or a meal whenever they were both in Panama City. That fateful holiday weekend in 2013, Francine and the Professor made plans to meet at a restaurant for dinner. Francine brought some friends with her; so did the Professor. Jack was one of those friends. He was in town from Baton Rouge, Louisiana, to play golf. By chance, Francine and the twice-divorced Jack sat at the same end of the table.

"I never intended for it to be a setup," the Professor told me, adding he was "pleasantly surprised" when he noticed a spark between them. It wasn't love at first sight, Francine said. Still, there was something there. "I got lucky," Jack said and laughed, as though he still couldn't believe just how lucky he'd gotten.

After dinner, the group went to a bar with live music. "Jack asked me to dance," Francine said. "I love to dance! But I find many men are too intimidated to dance. So I recognized confidence and a fun side of Jack that was appealing."

"I'm a horrible dancer," Jack said. "But after I turned fifty, my attitude was, screw it; I don't care. I don't care what people think about me anymore."

With heavy, unrelenting rain canceling the men's golf plans, the two friend groups hung out with each other all weekend. By the end of the holiday, Jack and Francine were making plans to see each other alone. They rendezvoused in New Orleans three weeks later and, "from that point on, we spent practically every weekend together," Francine said. "This was the most intense thing that I probably ever had experienced."

By November, Francine and Jack were planning a trip to Europe. "He had never been, and traveling is a big thing for me," Francine said. "I wanted to see how we traveled together. I have a theory: You need to be on a trip with someone for more than a week, just the two of you, and see how twenty-four hours a day together is going to work out."

It worked out. After a year of long-distance dating, Jack sold his home, took early retirement, and moved into Francine's place in Nashville. "I'd been with the same company for seventeen years," he said. "I had a very good job, and I loved what I did." But he'd never been a big fan of Baton Rouge and had always planned on retiring early anyway, knowing he could count on his frugality to see him through retirement years. Francine and Jack tied the knot in Nashville through a justice of the peace and later flew family and friends to Cuba to celebrate with a splashy reception.

As for the Professor, he told me he was happy to have inadvertently played a part in getting Francine and Jack together. "I tell them they're in my debt for the rest of their lives," he said, and when I teasingly suggested that maybe it was just for the rest of their marriage, he laughed loudly.

"That's right!" he said. "I take all of the credit for them getting together and if they break up, none of the blame."

∽⊗⊙∾

*From season 1's "Sex Talk" episode, the following is an excerpt of my inter-
view with Sandy, who got a gray divorce from the only person she'd ever had
sex with. She talked with me about how friends introduced her to the man
who became her second "first time."*

SANDY: For two years [after the divorce], I just was angry, and I knew
I would be a horrible partner, date—anything. It's like I just wanted to
work this out with myself and God, and grow up and figure out how I
was going to manage life by myself. And then after that I thought, *Well,
I should at least go date*. So I started online dating and, you know, met a
lot of really nice men. But I'd know immediately, *Nah*.

ME: Before you had ever been married, you wanted to save sex for that
special partner. Did you have the same attitude as an [older] single
woman, or were you even thinking about sex at this point?

SANDY: Yeah, that's funny. I wasn't thinking about having sex. You
know, when I first meet men, I'm thinking about, *Gosh, will I enjoy them?
Do I like them?*

ME: But then your friends introduced you to—can we give him a name?
Just to—so we're not calling him . . .

SANDY: Tom.

ME: Tom. Let's call him Tom.

SANDY: Tom. Okay.

ME: Okay. So friends introduced you?

SANDY: Yes. They invited me to dinner. And it, it was really weird. They
[also] invited my family—my sister, my-sister-in-law—and a bunch of
single women. Like it was *The Bachelor* or something.

ME: Ohhh. [Laughter]

SANDY: And I was so disgusted by the whole thing that I was like, *I'm
not even interested in talking to him*. I don't have a competitive bone in
my body.

ME: Wait, wait, wait, wait. I'm just trying to wrap my head around this:
Somebody becomes single, so family and friends throw him a dinner
party? And there's, like, all these potential people from whom he can
choose?

SANDY: Yeah. Yeah. It was gross. Fun for him.

ME: He was the only single guy?

SANDY: Yeah. He was late because he was buying roses for all of us. Just like, oh my God. [Laughter]

ME: It was *The Bachelor—The Gray Bachelor*! You went out to this dinner, but you were not competitive. So you kind of had a smirk on your face the whole time?

SANDY: I had no idea that three other women, eligible bachelorettes, were going to be there.

ME: Ohhhh. [Laughter]

SANDY: I thought it was going to be really casual.

ME: So you had dinner, you did go to the dinner and you got—apparently, you got *the* rose.

SANDY: He did call me [afterward] and asked me, you know, if I wanted to go out and watch a football game at a sports bar. I'm like, yeah, sure. It would be—that's safe territory.

Dear Laura,

Maybe six months after my former spouse left to be with another woman, a male friend raised [the idea of introducing me to] someone else. It was the furthest thing from my mind and frankly made me want to throw up. I'd dealt with everything: comforted the kids, sold the house in California, sold the house in D.C., sold the rentals, faced everyone in town one by one. I had zero interest in dating, so that's what I told him.

Several months later, my friend sent me and "the date guy" a group email saying we were two of his favorite people and we should get together for whatever. Intellectually, I was open to it; it was time. But I was shocked my friend sent the email without talking to me about it first.

The coffee, when it actually happened, was really important for me because I got [the first date after divorce] out of the way. I had the mindset that it was just like a business lunch, and I'm smart and funny and engaging in business lunches. And if something happens, it will be a seamless transition to dating. But it didn't go anywhere. The story is complicated, involving invitations I sent him with no response, including the time he showed up on my porch at the appointed day and time and, when I didn't answer his knock, realized he had failed to confirm. —M. K.

Hi Laura,
[After 14 years of marriage], I got divorced in 2001. Since that time I have been on and off dating sites and have tried to sign on with some dating services, often finding they have waiting lists for women. I have had a couple of relationships, but nothing for seven years. I'm 61, in great shape, am told I am a "great catch," and have a lot of friends and acquaintances, yet no one knows any single men. Don't all the men online have friends who have friends who know people I know? This is a mystery to me. —N., Washington, D.C.

CHAPTER EIGHT

~

Chance Encounters

About a year after inadvertently setting up his old friend Jack with his new friend Francine, the Professor was in Nepal on yet another international adventure. He'd spent large chunks of time exploring the world, finally able to act on the wanderlust that had been building since a short, troubled marriage had left him with sole custody of his young daughter.

"Here I am, a single dad in my late twenties with an eighteen-month-old," he recalled of those early years. "I could hardly take care of myself, much less a little girl. But I vowed that somehow we'd make it. And somehow, we did."

Juggling child-rearing and work, the Professor didn't have the time or inclination to date much. Many of the women he did meet wanted children of their own. "My goal was to get my child raised," he said. "I wasn't really in a financial position, or state of mind, to raise another one or have another one. I don't know if it was a mistake, but my daughter was the center of my life."

When his daughter left home for college, the Professor took early retirement. He went back to online dating—remember, that's how he met Francine—but basically struck out. Still, his life was full: skiing, sailing, skydiving, scuba diving in the Caribbean, hiking the Camino de Santiago, and visiting countries throughout Europe and South America.

Then came the trip to Nepal. the Professor was on a plane out of Kathmandu, and his seatmate was a Chinese woman a few years younger. Li didn't speak much English; the Professor didn't speak any Chinese. Despite the language barrier, they connected. The Professor learned Li was a successful business owner with grown kids, and she traveled occasionally to the United States. She'd be in California the following month, in fact. Maybe they could get together?

"I gave her my contact information, but I didn't think I would ever hear from her again," he recalled with a laugh. But Li did reach out, and the Professor invited her to swing by Florida. Thus began what might possibly be the longest distance long-distance relationship sparked by a chance meeting. As the Professor told me, "We're taking long-distance to the extreme."

Li had no interest in moving to the United States permanently; the Professor had no interest in moving to China. So they took turns living with each other and traveling together. Their routine was this: the Professor would spend six months in China, and then Li would spend six months in the United States. The relationship had found a good equilibrium.

"If life has taught me anything, it's to live in the moment without trying to predict the future or guide the future or even plan the future too much," the Professor told me. "You may have a direction for yourself, but there are detours along the way, and sometimes the detours can be more interesting than the road you'd planned to travel."

I absolutely adore hearing stories about random encounters that turn into gray romances. It's as if no matter what each person has experienced in the years before meeting each other, they are meant to be together from that moment on. Like Blair and Whitney, neighbors in a high-rise apartment building who introduced themselves to each other while aboard the complex's shuttle bus to the grocery store. "I was just kind of really taken by her beauty immediately," said Blair, a widower. As for Whitney, divorced and then in a fading long-distance relationship, "It sounds crazy; I just remember this jolt, like *Wow, wow—something about this man.*"

And Jeanne and Norm, two longtime singles after previous marriages and divorces. They met when musician Norm took an old guitar amp to the thrift store where musician Jeanne worked. "There's this room where they take donations, and the doorway had a curtain across it," Norm recalled. "I pulled the curtain back, and there's this smiley-face, gorgeous, twinkly-eyed woman sorting fabrics." Jeanne thought to herself, "Mmm, he could be a *Game of Thrones* extra!"

Then there was Steve, who literally almost backed into the woman who became his long-distance love while they were perusing opposite shelves in the travel section of a bookstore. After laughing it off, they struck up a conversation. "She asked me where in the world would I want to go. And I just sort of explained as I did a mental walk across the world," Steve told me. "And then before she left, she gave me her card. And one part of me was like, you know, *Do something different*—kind of in the same genre as forcing yourself to say yes instead of no. So . . . this couldn't have been more than five minutes later, I gave her a call."

I admit, as much as I enjoyed these kinds of stories, I also was envious. I mean, why couldn't *I* meet the next love of my life randomly? As a resident of the populous DMV, I had statistical opportunities that others didn't. Consider one divorced fifty-year-old woman in the Northeast. When she decided to go online, she set her search to up to a three-hour drive from her residence after realizing that in her tiny hometown, women outnumbered men by at least a factor of two.[1]

But of course, randomly connecting with someone requires not only having the opportunity but also seizing it. Looking up from my book to discover who's taken the seat on the plane next to me. Catching the eye of an interesting-looking stranger in a bookstore or thrift shop. Starting a conversation. Keeping it going. I didn't feel equipped. That's why I signed up for a ten-dollar "How to Flirt" online seminar with a relationship coach who billed herself as an expert on the topic. Let's call her Leigh.

This event wasn't advertised for women only or for young women only. Perhaps it should have been? Or maybe it was my mood on that particular evening. I found Leigh's hyper gender-normative approach surprising, given that she was about twenty-five years younger than I am and presumably more aware of speaking and acting in stereotypes. I also thought the presentation was tone deaf and borderline offensive.

Leigh said we shouldn't be selective about whom we choose to flirt with, and perhaps no one was flirting with us because "you have an F-U sign on your forehead." She suggested we hang out at bars and employ playful talk, such as calling a man's drink "girly" and telling him "you're bad" while touching his knee. When Leigh declared that "feminine power is essential to flirting," I submitted a question: "So when men flirt, does that mean they're using *their* feminine power?" My question went unanswered.

I found far greater insight through author Leslie Morgan Steiner, whose memoir *The Naked Truth* is about reclaiming her identity as a sexual being after a long and unfulfilling second marriage. Leslie intentionally spent a year having a lot of sex with a lot of men, no strings attached. I wasn't looking to do the same, necessarily, but I was impressed by Leslie's ability to meet so many willing partners. (She doesn't drink alcohol, so she wasn't sitting on barstools touching men's knees and making fun of their beverages.)

At the end of the book, Leslie offers what she calls a cheat sheet— advice for sparking seemingly random connections. Her tips included locking eyes with every person who catches your interest and making yourself easy to approach. "Men are *everywhere*. In airports, restaurants, the supermarket, Starbucks, yoga class, the local dog park . . . you name it," Leslie writes. "But you have to see them. And make them see you."[2]

I invited Leslie to the WAMU studio in Washington, D.C., to talk more about chance encounters for season 1's "Brand-New Day" episode. Here's part of our conversation on that frigid late afternoon in December 2019:

> ME: I belong to a running group. I go out to the movies. I go out with my friends. I go to a church. I feel like either out of habit or maybe nervousness, I don't scan the room, so to speak. Tell me what to do.
>
> LESLIE: So this is what you have to do. First, you have to see the people who are already there. Then you have to understand what you like and have faith in your judgment. Once you start to trust that you do have this inner picker that works, then you get to the part that I think is really hard—which is, when you see somebody you like, you've got to go talk to them. And that's what we women have a very hard time doing because we're not taught to do it. Men are taught to do it from the time they're twelve years old.
>
> You know, we have a lot of ability to communicate with people without using words. Is the person turning toward you or turning away from you? Are they buried in their phone, or are they smiling back at you?

And I will go on those cues. And if the person seems like they're open the way that I am, and friendly, I will strike up a conversation.

And then you just wait and see. Is the conversation going smoothly? Is there an easy way to say, "Oh, here's my card; I'd love to, you know, have coffee some time"? It's easier than you think, once you get into the groove.

After our sit-down, Leslie and I ventured outside, accompanied by podcast producer Ruth lugging recording equipment. Leslie wanted to play a game she calls Yes or No. The purpose was to, one, open my eyes to the reality that I cross paths on any given day with several men and, two, get in the habit of making a quick decision about whether I'd theoretically want to strike up any conversations.

The three of us planted ourselves on a Connecticut Avenue street corner, near the Giant grocery store and the staircase for the Van Ness-UDC Metro train. Then we started playing. The man clutching a stuffed grocery bag at its twisted neck instead of carrying it? He was a no because, snap judgment, anyone holding a bag like that must be a weirdo. Another no from me for the slender youth wearing a nylon tracksuit, because he couldn't have been older than twenty-one. (Linc and Sunny would have been mortified!) He earned a yes from Leslie, though. "I love young," she explained. "And obviously he's an athlete." Besides, she reminded me, I wasn't trying to discern if someone was husband material or not. Old habits . . .

The man with scruffy facial hair? Yes. The man with the meticulously groomed moustache and beard . . . no. The hatless bald guy, yes. The hatless bald guy with a comb-over? No. The rumpled man exiting the Metro who looked down at his phone after making eye contact? He got a no from Leslie: "Why waste time pursuing someone who's clearly not interested?" However, I hesitated before declaring, "He's a maybe." Rumpled Man appeared to be age-appropriate. The rumpledness looked like it was from the end of a long and productive day and not general sloppiness. Also, there was something about the way he was looking at his phone that didn't seem authentic to me—like he was pretending to look at it but really, he was more interested in us.

Maybe he was shy, I decided. Maybe he wanted to talk but, like me, had trouble approaching intriguing strangers.

Leslie and I continued playing the Yes or No game; a minute or so later, I looked over my shoulder. A few feet away was Rumpled Man, only pretending—I was sure now—to read his phone while actually watching us.

"Leslie, look," I said. "I'm turning my maybe into a yes."

An unexpected development in our little game: possibly making a connection! "Catch his eye, and give him a big smile," Leslie excitedly advised me. "Let's see what happens."

I turned and looked directly at Rumpled Man, smiling until he lifted both eyes completely from his phone and tentatively smiled back. Woot! Then he put his phone in his pocket and walked over. Leslie was practically jumping with glee.

"Hi!" I chirped. "I'm Laura!"

"Hi," he responded, not as brightly. "I noticed your recording equipment and was wondering if something was happening that I should be aware of. I'm [Recognizable Media Name]."

Damn. Rumpled Man's curiosity was purely professional. Plus, when he heard what we were doing, he quickly volunteered that he was married. I got kudos from Leslie for my instincts and also for my effort. Alas, no love connection either with Rumpled Man (obviously) or with the single friend he helpfully tried connecting me with later that evening via email. Dude never responded. His loss.

After the episode aired, I got a scolding from a listener who said Leslie's advice to randomly approach strangers and hand over business cards was dangerous. Still, playing the Yes or No game had energized me. I made a New Year's resolution to really put myself out there starting in 2020, in the hopes of making a love connection. The pandemic put the kibosh on that plan, of course. As of this writing, though, almost two years have passed since Leslie and I played the game, and I am not only fully vaccinated but also boosted. Full immunity, baby! Time to make another resolution and stick with it.

⌒∞⌒

If I had met this man on a dating site, I doubt I would have gone out with him. I have a master's degree; he has a high school education and has been my auto mechanic for at least five years. We never conversed other than about whatever vehicle I had brought in. My eleven-year relationship broke up, and I was doing the Internet dating thing, but he was in the back of my mind. I had my car in his shop one day, and we started chatting. He offered to come to my house and fix my lawnmower. I have never felt so loved in my life. What he has to offer, I never found in any man who fit my checklist. So throw those darn lists away! You never know. —K. G.

Loved your podcast. I'm sharing it with everyone! Where can I find a picture of Blair and Whitney? I'm dying to see what they look like. —B. B.

After dates last fall with eight nice women, none of which resulted in any second dates, I met someone who is still around four months later. We met at a coffee shop (her version and true) but we learned about each other on a dating website. —R. B.

Hello Laura,
I was married for twenty-three years to my first husband, and we had an extremely fulfilling life together until his passing in 2004. It was nearly seven years before I considered dating. I decided to ask my accountant of twenty-plus years to go out with me. I approached him the first time through a thank-you card after the 2011 tax-filing season. He did not respond. I asked him to go out with me again through another thank-you card after the 2012 tax-filing season. I heard back from him about seven months later. We had an amazing courtship of about eleven months as we learned about each other. We got married in December 2013, two wedding ceremonies: the first a surprise ceremony [overseas], and the second in my family's home where I grew up. —A. K. T.

I feel drawn to tell you that last spring, I was out walking in a neighborhood I'd never walked in before, about a quarter-mile from my home.
A woman went by me on rollerblades. She was athletic and pretty and
had a long black braid down her back. Then she came by me again but
actually stopped on the road next to me this time. Now, I tend toward
shyness and being socially awkward at times, especially if I'm taken by
surprise. Even though I was glad she stopped to talk, I was tongue-tied.

We traveled down to the end of the road together, and then there was
an awkward pause—like, what now? I was self-conscious because I was so
attracted to her and very aware of being single and wishing for a woman
to date, so I was scared I'd seem desperate if I asked her if she wanted to
walk together some time. I stood there, frozen, as she muttered goodbye
and then rolled away.

Why didn't I say something else?! Why didn't I ask her if she wanted
to walk again? Or her name? Or something?! I just stood there, watching
her roll away from me. In the distance, she turned all the way around
in a circle and looked back at me. She looked disappointed, yet I still
did nothing. The movie of that moment has played over and over in my
mind ever since. What was wrong with me?! I'm feeling extra lonely and
sad at my lost opportunity. —Shelly, North Carolina

PART III

KEEPING

CHAPTER NINE

~

Past Is Present

The biggest buzz at my high school class reunion was not about the formerly hunky athlete who'd grown up to look almost exactly like character actor Ed Asner, aka Mr. Grant on *The Mary Tyler Moore Show*. Instead, it was over how much time Heather and Brad were spending alone together talking, their gracefully aging bodies pressed close so they could hear each other above the cheerfully rowdy crowd in the reunion hotel ballroom.

Tall, lithe, and golden-haired, Heather and Brad had been the "it" couple in the class of 1978. They'd broken up to attend different colleges and then live full lives: marriages, kids, still-thriving careers. Forty years later, rumor had it they were both single again. Would they end the evening making out? Fall madly in love again and—ooh, ooh—figure out a way to be together despite the fourteen-hundred-mile distance between their respective hometowns?

Yes, I was acting like a silly teenager all over again. (When time traveling in Rome, and all that.) In my defense, though, there was science behind the seemingly magical appeal of reconnecting romantically with someone from the past.

"My . . . years of research have led me to believe that rekindled romances are not uncommon but are simply one of the many ways people find love," California-based psychology professor Nancy Kalish wrote in *Lost and Found Lovers*.[1] Nancy built an entire career on this topic. Before sharing her findings, however, I feel like I should go on the record on this subject and state that since splitting with Lex, I have been in contact with my high school boyfriend. Several years ago, C. randomly emailed to ask if he could call after work to talk about an idea he had for a creative project. Curious, I responded with yes and my cell phone number. It just so happened to be my birthday. C. didn't remember this; turned out, it also was his brother's birthday, a shared-day fact neither of us had recalled.

On the phone that evening, C. told me that for the past couple of years he had been mulling over writing a book based on a little-known but riveting sporting event to which he had personal ties. C.'s career was in finance, so writing this book would basically be an unfamiliar labor of love squeezed into his precious spare time. I was the only writer he knew, so my potential evaluation had been on his mind. (I agreed: It was a book-worthy topic.) Then, that morning—my birthday morning, remember—he'd woken up with an unexplainable feeling he should reach out.

Now, before you get all excited, C. also mentioned that he talked to his wife about getting in touch with me, and she was fine with it. So I knew right away C. wasn't attempting to reconnect romantically; he really did want my professional opinion. I took the experience as a sign from my dad, who had died six months earlier. Dad was letting me know that someone who'd once been very important in my life was thinking about me positively, and also that it was okay I had been upset about Lex's secret friendship with Mona. As C. demonstrated by sharing that his wife was aware he'd be calling, a person who cared about their partner's feelings didn't hide their actions involving other people.

I heard again from still-happily-married C. at the end of 2020, when he texted his condolences after learning through mutual friends that my mom had died. And that has been the extent of our communication, as it probably should be for his continued matrimonial harmony.

Back to Nancy's research. In 2003 on NPR's *Weekend Edition*, she had explained the appeal of what I call boomerang relationships. "[They] were couples in their formative years. They went to school together. They grew up together. They knew each other's families. And together, they actually defined what love is," she said. "And it's a very comforting and familiar sensation to see these people again."[2]

Nancy added: "The other thing—which I don't do research on but I know about—is the physiology of this. These first loves may actually be hardwired in the brain as a memory of sensations: touch, smell, hearing. And these memories all come back when you see that person again."[3]

Nancy would know. In the early 1990s she reconnected romantically with her college sweetheart. Things didn't work out on that second go-around either, but the experience had prompted her to initiate a research undertaking she christened the Lost Love Project. She spent the next quarter century surveying people all over the world, writing books and research papers, and establishing a website where people could join forums to talk about their experiences making love reconnections. Sadly, Nancy had a heart attack and died in 2019 at the age of seventy-two.

Nancy's research included lost lovers of all ages. She found that the majority reconnect with a love from high school or junior high, while about 29 percent reunite with a love from the college-age years of eighteen to twenty-two. People ages sixty-five and older are more likely to seek out "puppy loves"—preteen childhood crushes. Nancy found that as people grew older, they are less likely to seek out a reconnection. But if they do reach out, their success rate for a lasting reconnection increases.[4]

Overall, Nancy found, couples who get back together have good odds for making it work for the long haul—anywhere between 72 and 78 percent, depending on the stage of life when the first connection was made. But there's a caveat: Successful recoupling doesn't rely on geography but on both people being legally available when they find each other again.[5]

"It doesn't matter if they're on opposite coasts or even different countries," said Jeannie Thompson, a mental-health counselor and advocate who has led discussion groups on the website Nancy founded. Jeannie and I talked for the "Boomerang Love" episode during season 2 of *Dating While Gray*. "There's nothing that will stop them from finding a way to be together if they're both available," she added.

Like John and Valerie, who shared their story with *Washington Post* columnist John Kelly. John and Valerie had dated in high school, but just before graduating in 1970, they broke up over a misunderstanding. (Valerie heard a rumor that John had been falsely bragging about how far they'd gone sexually.) They'd each gotten married and had kids, then had a quick convo at their twentieth high school reunion but otherwise, had no contact. Another dozen years would pass before the now-divorced Valerie ran into the now-divorced John virtually when she logged onto a new high school alumni website. Valerie commented on John's post, John responded, and soon they were talking on the phone and getting the air cleared. (Back in the day, John explained, he hadn't known there was a difference between the phrases "making *out*" and "making *love*.") After their second phone call in two days, New Hampshire resident John asked if he could visit Valerie in Colorado. She said yes. They've been back together ever since, living in Colorado and married for more than a decade now.[6]

Here's what I found super interesting about Nancy's project: She gathered data from both sides of the line marking the digital age. When she first started her project, she probably couldn't have predicted how technology would enhance information gathering. Now that home computers, smartphones, and Googling are ubiquitous, who among us has never clicked around a bit to try to find out what an old flame is up to?

"If we're married for a period of time, maybe it's lost some of the zing that was there. We aren't investing as much in the relationship as we could be," Jeannie Thompson told me. "And so it's lost some of the excitement, some of the connection, and we're kind of missing that. And we start to look back: *I remember that time I was crazy in love with that person. I wonder what happened to them.* And then we start getting those reunion letters and emails and invitations and it's like, *Oh, my gosh,* you know? And so then that kind of triggers everything for us to take another look back at . . . the one who got away."

Pre–digital age, people looking to reconnect not only had to make a much bigger effort, but they also probably had to be more open about their search: for example, making telephone calls or writing letters of inquiry to family members or friends of the lost love. And thus, according to Nancy, the majority making love reconnections in those years were divorced, widowed, or otherwise available to recouple.

Not so for the Googlers of the digital age. Nancy found that the majority of people who go online to successfully reconnect are married or their lost love is. Or they both are! With these types of reconnections, Nancy uncovered only a 5 percent chance of a happily ever after for the lost loves.[7] Not that they aren't thrilled to see each other again or instantly attracted. It's that their reconnection is more likely to lead to an emotional or physical affair but not a split from the partner to whom they are already committed.

If either party is married, "Definitely don't make contact," Jeannie advised. "That was something [Nancy] was very, very clear about. And I have to reiterate that. It's the highest high you'll ever feel. But there's also the lowest low, the greatest pain and despair that you'll ever experience."

Jeannie spoke from experience. She'd come across Nancy's lost love website after trying to heal emotionally from her own reconnection with her high school boyfriend. Back in the day, Jeannie and her beau had tried to make it work even after going to different colleges. They wound up breaking up and then lost touch. The memories, however, persisted.

"I kept all the letters and mementos from that time we were together; I kept everything," Jeannie recalled. "And I always wondered, *Where is he? What's he doing?* And one day [in the early 2000s] I found out about Google—and there you have it. There was a picture of him, and I tell you, I almost fainted. You know, over the years I kind of looked for him in crowds. And there he was on a screen right in front of my face. I contacted him via an email that I found online. And a few days later, I got an email back."

Jeannie was married. So was her former sweetheart. Still, they spent about three months talking online before making a plan to meet in person on their anniversary as a high school couple. That day, they drove separately to a park. Jeannie arrived first. "I saw his car pull up, and I could see him walking from his car to where I was in the park," she recalled. "My heart is pounding out of my chest; all I wanted to do was grab him. As we hugged I said, 'I forgot how tall you are.' He said, 'I forgot how short you are.'"

They took a stroll around the lake before having dinner at a nearby restaurant. "He sat across the table from me. And he's looking at me, and I'm looking at him, and he said, 'I have to move. I'm too far away from you.' And he moved to the seat next to me." Sigh.

"He kept every letter I wrote while he was in college, and on the day we met, he gave me all of them," Jeannie said wistfully. "And he still had a bottle of my perfume from thirty-five years ago. It was almost overwhelming to realize he still had feelings for me all these years later, even though we both have lived other lives."

Jeannie and her lost love communicated online off and on for a year or so after that meeting. But they never saw each other again. Jeannie ended contact after realizing their secret relationship undoubtedly was interfering with their respective marriages. That was ten years ago. As far as Jeannie knew when we talked, he was still married. Jeannie, however, wound up getting divorced. Another sigh!

Some people may not need the aid of the Internet to figure out what their former flame is up to because their former flame is a public figure. A New York Times article describes the following story: When Edwin was on the debate team in high school, he started dating Donna, a girl from a competing school's team. Edwin and Donna continued to date their freshman year at the same college, then broke up. Edwin went on to law school and became an attorney in California. Donna got an advanced journalism degree and became an actress and television personality based in New York. They both got married to other people and then got divorced. Donna was married and divorced twice, in fact. Her second husband, of eighteen years, was Rudy Giuliani. Donna had been first lady of the Big Apple when Rudy was mayor.

About a year after Donna and Rudy split, Edwin made contact for the first time since he and Donna had broken up all those decades ago. He telephoned Donna to ask if she'd be attending their thirtieth college reunion. That phone call changed everything. Edwin and Donna got together even before the reunion, and a year after that they walked down the aisle. As of this writing, a happily ever after.[8]

Some boomerang connections occur between people who were never romantically involved with each other. Washington Post writer Lisa Bonos shared the story of Betty and Peter. Back in high school, they knew each other because Betty had dated Peter's best friend and Peter had dated Betty's. After graduation in the late '60s they'd lost touch and built separate lives. Both had gotten married and then divorced. Peter wound up living on a houseboat in California, while Betty stayed in their shared Virginia childhood hometown.

More than fifty years after high school, they found and friended each other on Facebook. When Peter traveled to Virginia to visit his parents, he met up with Betty. Their friendship reconnection was instant; it deepened through phone calls and emails after Peter returned to California. When the COVID-19 pandemic hit and quarantining was imminent, Betty decided it was time to let Peter know how she really felt. She wrote him an email with the subject line "The Teen-Age Betty in Me Confesses."

Betty told Peter she "wasn't planning on really liking you—but I do . . . and when you like someone, you worry about their safety. Please, please take this quarantining seriously. . . . In the meantime, I will work on liking you less so you won't think I am . . . crazy . . ."[9]

That message was all Peter needed. He decided to spend concentrated time in Virginia. He'd be closer to his parents, and he and Betty would be able to explore their connection IRL. The plan was for Peter to stay in Betty's guest bedroom, and he did. For one night. Then he moved into Betty's room to share her bed. More than a year later, they're still together in Betty's home, and Peter is planning to sell his houseboat. "Sometimes good friendships very unexpectedly develop into much more," Betty wrote on her Facebook page announcing their new relationship status.[10]

Grace and Scott's reconnection story was messier. It sounded sweet to those who knew them as high school friends and neighbors in Virginia in the '70s. It was horrifying to those who knew Grace with Walt, her husband of thirty years, and their three kids in Texas.

"Everyone in Virginia thinks it's so romantic Scott and I got together," Grace told me over lunch one day, prepandemic. "And everyone in Texas thinks I'm a whore."

Grace, sixty-one, spoke candidly and humorously about her experience, but even now the anguish she still felt about hurting Walt and their grown kids was palpable. She was finally feeling emotionally healthy, and Walt had a gray romance of his own after their split and had remarried. Still, Grace had regrets. "If I had truly thought about what divorce really meant, what relationships would really suffer, if I had just been more clear-headed, maybe I would have asked for just a time-out from Walt, maybe a little separation," Grace told me.

Grace was far from thinking clearly on that night in December 2009 when childhood neighbor Scott reached out with a seemingly innocent Facebook message: "Hey, remember me?" She had lost thirty pounds she hadn't needed to lose, was drinking wine like it was water, and "popping Xanax like there was no tomorrow," she said. Her youngest child had left the nest, and "I had turned into the caricature of the woman who hits menopause and empty nest at the same time and just loses her frickin' mind."

Grace had met Walt, the man who went on to become her first husband, on the day she'd arrived at college. Walt was a senior; they'd clicked instantly. Grace left school and married Walt after he'd finished his mechanical engineering degree. He was twenty-four, analytical and practical, and kept his feelings buttoned up tightly. Grace was nineteen, creative and emotional, a right-brained to his left-brained thinker.

"He's a real caretaker," Grace said, "and a good, good man. But our personalities are so different. Plus, nineteen is just too young to get married. There was one moment on our honeymoon when we were walking along the beach and I got physically ill because I started thinking, *What have I done?*"

Grace and Walt had a daughter and two sons while his job took them all over the world. They were living in Saudi Arabia when the first Persian Gulf War broke out. Grace begged her husband to pack up the family and return to the United States. He refused, calmly noting the chances of a Scud missile hitting their home were infinitesimal.

"It was statistical odds compared to emotion, fear, panic," Grace recalled. "Every night the siren would go off, and I'd grab all three kids and go hide in the closet. That's when something kind of shifted in me. They became *my* kids, and I no longer trusted anyone else to make decisions regarding what was best for them." She later was diagnosed with post-traumatic stress.

After Saudi Arabia, the family settled in Texas. With Walt frequently traveling for work, Grace threw herself headlong into parenting, and along the way, she lost herself. "We've been hearing about men who become unhappy at midlife for a really long time," she reflected. "But women just usually drown themselves in eating and drinking and shopping. You know, I spent a lot of years doing something very important to me: I successfully raised my children to leave home, and the thanks I get is they did!"

Grace continued: "A lot of my peer group at the time were kind of going through the same thing. But their children married younger than mine and started having children. I watched in envy and panic as I saw [other long-married women] soothe whatever angst or discontent they were having by becoming grandparents and filling the void with that."

Then Scott randomly reached out. Did Grace remember him? Did she ever. "He was so cool" when he was younger, Grace recalled. "He had long hair and played the guitar—I had such a crush. We'd never dated at all, so this seemed like it was just the fantasy I was looking for."

Scott and Grace spent about a month pouring their hearts out to each other online. Scott sounded miserable too. Married and divorced twice, he was living unhappily with a volatile girlfriend and their teenaged daughter in the DMV. He had already left once. He promised his daughter he'd never leave again. He was regretting the vow.

After the Christmas holidays, Grace drove from Texas to the DMV to rendezvous with Scott. She stayed at the home of her parents, who were spending the winter in Florida. Scott came over shortly after she arrived in town. They wound up sitting on the sofa for hours, talking and snuggling.

"It was like reuniting, even though we had never been a couple in high school," she told me. After three days together, they became physical. Moreover, Scott was proclaiming his love for her. Part of Grace hesitated. Another part was thrilled. "It was so exciting," Grace said. "It was like, *This must be the thing that's missing, the thing that's going to make me happy.*"

Grace returned to Texas with no plans to end either her affair or her marriage. The friends turned lovers had another secret meeting. Only a few months later, they were discovered. Grace's son Bryce and his wife had moved back into the Texas family home temporarily after an overseas work assignment. Bryce and Grace had always been close, and he immediately sensed something was up. After putting spyware on his mother's computer, he had proof.

Bryce confronted Grace, threatening to tell his dad if Grace didn't end the affair. Instead, Grace told Walt about it herself and then moved out of their family home and into their vacation cottage nearby.

Walt, emotionally reeling, asked Grace to see a marriage counselor with him. She refused. Bryce stopped speaking to Grace; her daughter and other son were dumbfounded and devastated.

Meanwhile, Grace and Scott continued their relationship. Eventually, Scott extricated himself from his other romantic entanglement. He bought a house near the one he'd been sharing with his girlfriend and daughter, and Grace moved in with him. For the next few years, she traveled to Texas frequently to try to repair her relationships with her sons and her daughter, who was now a mother herself.

Grace and Walt officially divorced in November 2011, and about two and a half years later Grace and Scott got married in a simple backyard ceremony. "I don't want to fail again," Grace said, "and we both want to stay together." Still, gray romance can be tricky. Grace may have been frustrated and even bored by Walt's slow and steady nature, but she was frequently caught off guard by Scott's fiery, excitable, and sometimes irrational behavior. She also found it difficult to trust him.

"Scott was a lousy husband to his two wives, and he was a lousy partner to the mother of his child," Grace said. "In our darkest fights, I tell him that I married him to punish myself. I did it because I didn't think I deserved anything better. It's beyond cruel."

But Grace said Scott has been a better partner than she'd given him credit for, and he proved he is committed to her. He retired early, and they moved to Texas to live full-time so that Grace could be near her kids and grandchildren. Grace has mended her relationship with all of them, even Bryce after he went through the trauma of his own marital split. "I wish that hadn't happened to him," she said, "but his heart softened to me."

By the time we talked, Grace sounded philosophical about the path she'd taken to be with Scott. "In many ways, it's been a real relief to have fallen on my face," she said. "It took a load off of me. I'm not angry anymore. And I'm not judging other people anymore. I have empathy and sympathy for people who commit wrongs."

She also recognized that relationships that start in deceit—like hers and Scott's—rarely have happy endings, as Nancy Kalish identified with the 5 percent success rate. With that in mind, Grace hopes her gray romance will be a cautionary tale for others who might face similar situations. "If you know yourself, move forward. Make sure you're thinking clearly. And if you are, then trust your instincts," she advised. "But if you aren't, slow down and do what you need to do to think clearly. Don't do anything you can't undo."

Finally, there is one other variation of love reconnection that I came across in my research: two people who weren't just in love but were married and then split up before eventually finding their way back together. One such couple was Linda and Peter. They met in college and walked down the aisle shortly after graduation. For the next thirty-five-plus years, they climbed their respective career ladders and raised two sons. Things started to fall apart when the boys were grown and gone. That was around the same time Peter was diagnosed with heart disease. Instead of turning to his wife for emotional support, he withdrew. A few years after quadruple bypass surgery, the couple separated, and a few years after that their divorce was finalized.[11]

Linda and Peter remained friendly while attempting to make new romantic connections through online dating. Three years after their divorce was final, both of their sons became engaged. Linda and Peter started spending more time together to meet their sons' pending in-laws and help with wedding plans. Soon they were having heartfelt conversations about their own marriage and where things had gone sideways. "It's never too late to live happily ever after," Linda told a New York Times reporter after walking down the aisle with Peter again, in December 2019.[12]

A couple in Denmark, Kjeld and Lotte, had been married for twenty-four years before divorcing in 1989. They'd lived separately for only twenty-four months before getting back together. Twenty-nine years later, in the midst of the coronavirus pandemic, Kjeld and Lotte officially became husband and wife again. "They knew the virus could be lethal to both of them," one of their four grown children, Simon, told a Washington Post reporter. "The risk of either of them leaving the world without officially becoming husband and wife was something they could not accept."[13]

I interviewed another such couple, Mary and Del, for season 2 of Dating While Gray. They'd been married for twenty years—a second marriage for each—but things had gone stale. In fact, they hadn't had sex for more than a decade, at Del's refusal. Del didn't want to talk about it. Mary was confused and hurt, especially after Del had twice openly flirted with and romantically kissed other women at parties the couple had attended.

"I didn't think that he was having affairs," Mary told me. "But I did think it's a pretty aggressive act to kiss another woman in front of your wife. I did say things like, 'Can you explain to me why this is happening?'"

Del wouldn't, or couldn't. Then suddenly one day he announced not only was he leaving, but he was also planning to force the sale of their home so they each could comfortably settle somewhere else. "You asked if we were happy," Del circled back to one of my questions. "In many ways, we were happy. We were deeply in love with each other. We respected each other. We trusted each other. We had good times. But we also had troubles. And I was having a hard time . . . getting a clear picture of it. So I started to feel—and this is odd or unusual to say—but I felt like I needed to be outside the relationship in order to see things clearly."

Del insisted he didn't want to get divorced; he just needed time by himself. Mary, understandably confused and distraught, started seeing a therapist and bought a condo. "I bought in the same neighborhood," Del said.

"And I'm thinking, *What is he doing?*" Mary told me. "*He wants to be away from me, and he's bought a condo three blocks away from me!*"

Mary also tried online dating in hopes of finding a new romantic partner. "I just didn't understand [what was going on with Del], and he wasn't explaining. And when you're surrounded by this kind of silence at the same time I'm being told it's really not my fault . . . and I figure, *Well, isn't that what everybody says when they break up*—'It's not your fault'? I just, you know, I just need to move on."

Mary added, "But I would say this: I never shut the door on him. I never said to him, 'I don't ever want to talk to you.'"

In fact, Mary turned to Del when a man she'd broken up with after dating briefly wouldn't take "no" for an answer. First, the man had showed up at a creative writing class Mary was teaching at the Smithsonian. Then Mary had noticed him at the local restaurant where she and her book group had gathered for their meeting. She'd been getting ready to leave and was suddenly afraid of walking home alone. "I get on my cell phone and call Del," Mary said. "And I tell him, 'I don't understand what's happening, but I need someone to walk me home.'"

Del had dropped whatever he was doing and within minutes had arrived at the restaurant to escort Mary safely home. "At that moment, I knew that maybe we'll never get back together again," Mary told me, "but this is the man I trust."

During their separation, Del and Mary shared a joint banking account with no issues and meanderingly worked on a property-settlement agreement. Del, too, received therapy. "I learned a lot about myself," he said. "But I also learned a lot about who I needed, who I wanted to be with. And I knew that I had the person I wanted to be with for the rest of my life."

Finally, one day after four years' separation, Del approached Mary and said he was ready to talk through their problems and work things out. It's a long story, but they've been reunited now for more than a decade. Here's an excerpt from our conversation on the season 2 podcast episode "Boomerang Love":

> DEL: I always felt through all of this that we would get back together. And I would tell her this, much to her exasperation, but I really believed it. I knew I might lose her through this process but I thought that I have to do this in order to—to somehow fix this and bring it back together better than it was.
>
> In fact, Laura, something that you said on—I think it was on your first [podcast episode] really resonated with me.
>
> ME: Okay.
>
> DEL: You said, "Maybe I wasn't whole when I was married. But now, years later, I'm whole now." And that's—my process was very complex and very deep, and it's hard to describe in twenty-five words or less. But if one can describe it in a sentence, that describes it.
>
> MARY: There are a lot of steps that were involved. And I'm not saying that [getting back together] just magically happened. But it does feel magical and miraculous to me. And I think that's the way love ought to be.

Truthfully, I hesitated to share Del and Mary's reconnection love story—or, really, any story involving estranged spouses who reunite. Perhaps it's because I vividly remember those two years after Lex and

I split but before we got divorced. I looked at his inaction on making the split legal as a hopeful sign rather than seeing it for what it was: indecisiveness and ambivalence. I understand now that I wanted my marriage to work not necessarily because it was the good and right thing for either of us personally but because Lex and I had history.

Also, frankly, I was terrified of being on my own. Weren't husbands and wives supposed to stick it out until we died? I remember desperately looking for answers by reading countless relationship-advice books, including Iris Krasnow's *Secret Lives of Wives: Women Share What It Really Takes to Stay Married*. Not once had I considered that the word *happily* was absent from Iris's title. Now, years later, I wondered. Not to pass judgment on the decisions other people made, but was "staying" married a laudable goal for longtime married couples even after any kids have grown and left home and with no consideration of personal happiness, independence, or growth? What would have happened had Mary connected with one of her online dates or if Del had ventured to look around romantically? Why did Mr. T, from season 2's "Love in the Stars" episode, privately refer to his supposedly unhappy marriage as his "lot in life" rather than doing something—anything!—to either make it better or to end it? Was the devil you knew, so to speak, better than the devil you didn't know or, hey, better than being alone?

Getting back together with my ex-husband—that kind of boomerang love is not in the cards for me, and I am now perfectly fine with that. My high school boyfriend, C., also is not a romantic candidate—not as long as he's married, anyway. I'm fine with that too. But I do like thinking about a pool of potential partners among anyone I ever knew when I was younger. And here's where I tell you that since getting divorced, I've gone out on dates with four boys—well, men now—from my high school. Four! One was a coincidence; we found out we had gone to the same high school on our first and only get-together. The other three I ran into online or met at various alumni events. No lasting romantic connections but, hey, it was a big school. And I haven't even tried tapping into the potential pool from my college alma mater. Not yet anyway.

⸎

Hello Laura,

I have heard stories by others who have reconnected after much time with someone they had a relationship with years ago. I have a love/hate relationship with this kind of story because, for some reason, the guys who have resurfaced in my life have not been the ones I have wanted to hear from. Instead I've gotten what I find to be irritating letters from guys I was relieved to have shaken loose from decades ago. Narcissists, sociopaths, clueless romantics. (Thanks, Internet, for giving my address away.)

Now, about my cousin. Some years ago while living in Berlin, her 50th high school reunion was being planned in Cleveland Heights, Ohio. She got an email from her high school sweetheart saying he was sorry to find out she wouldn't be attending. One email one day was followed by three the next day, ten the next day. . . . Eventually my cousin and this fellow got together and wrote a novel inspired by their experience. My fiftieth is scheduled for this summer. I go to each one without expectations. —D. L.

Hi there,

I found out a former college boyfriend was now divorced and saw him in Chicago two years ago. We text about once a month, but he doesn't want a relationship evidently. I can't figure men out!!! BTW I just turned 60 and am financially secure. I am happy with my life, good friends, health, and stability. But once you've had that one person who "gets" you, it's hard to live your life without that. I liked one of your statements, that finding love takes time. I just don't know where to look. —M. R.

Hi Laura!

I recently reconnected via IM, text, and phone with a fellow I dated when we were both 22, up in Massachusetts, where I'm from. Remembering the hot thang we had for each other over thirty-six years ago seems to have awakened a lone, barely glowing coal still in the hibachi within my long-abandoned libidinal she-shack (for want of a better expression). I have not been on a date, let alone gotten laid, since 7/2/2011. —E. B.

One [old girlfriend] said something that stuck with me for decades. She observed that I had the unpleasant habit of failing to finish many of the things I had started. At the age of 68, I graduated cum laude with a B.A. in English. I did some sleuthing and came up with a cell phone number for her. I took a photo of my diploma and texted it to her. If her path crossed mine, I would certainly greet her. But I am otherwise not interested. —J. B.

A few years ago, my first (ex) wife and I were both dating people we'd dated in high school. Our kids thought it was hysterical! —Larry

A little Internet searching provided some surprising results. Several women I had dated or had at least known and been attracted to had passed away, including one at age 43 and another at 51. I found that rather sad. The others were, and I suppose still are, married. I will not go there! —B. W.

Hmmm . . . I've often wondered. —T. L.

I reconnected with an old boyfriend from high school. The spark was still there, but I was happily married; he was not. Ten years later, my husband left me for a woman who he'd gone to college with. She found him on Facebook (Thanks, Zuckerberg). I was completely blindsided. When I reconnected with the old boyfriend again, he had divorced and remarried, with two little kids. Now I'm remarried, and he's divorced again and in poor health. I realize now that if [we'd both been available at the same time], we probably would not have had an ideal relationship. We don't have similar outlooks or values. It makes me very sad to see how bitter he's become, worn down by circumstances, whereas I'm much more resilient. —L. W.

Earlier this year, a college crush looked me up. It was thrilling for both of us to reconnect after failed marriages and to find the attraction was as strong as ever. We had a whirlwind romance—and little by little I realized that the issues/differences that I didn't care much about or notice in college were suddenly deal breakers. —Linda

My current romance is a "boomerang" relationship. Sweeter, so far, the second time around! —A. W.

CHAPTER TEN

~

Redefining Happily Ever After

When Helen Fisher got married more than a half century after her first trip down the aisle, perhaps no one was more surprised than she was. It wasn't that Helen, then seventy-five, didn't love journalist John Tierney, then sixty-seven. She'd known him professionally for twenty years before they'd formed a friendship that turned into a friends with benefits situation and then a committed relationship.[1] Helen just hadn't seen any point in making their commitment legal.

"I got married when I was twenty-three, and I was married for only about four months," Helen told me. "I didn't want to marry that man . . . but I was so scared of my mother that I did it anyway. And then we very rapidly got a divorce."

In the decades that followed, Helen had two committed but not wedded partnerships. One lasted about fifteen years, the other eighteen. Meanwhile, Helen built her career as probably *the* premier expert on the brain science behind romantic love. After Helen and John's professional relationship became personal, they dated for about six months before the twice-divorced John ended things in November 2015, fearing they'd become too serious. Helen was heartbroken, but she mourned privately.[2] Several weeks later, John got back in touch and asked for another chance. A few weeks into the New Year, they were back together, a committed couple maintaining separate residences.

John's son started college eighteen months later; subsequently, John proposed to Helen. "I thought it was charming," she told me. Still, she hesitated. "I said, 'Sweetheart, you don't have to marry me. I'm going to leave you everything I've got. I'm dedicated to you for the rest of my life. I'm done with sleeping around; that's all over for me.' I mean, I'm crazy about him in every way. But I didn't see the merit of actually marrying him." After realizing how important marriage was to the more traditional-minded John, though, Helen agreed—with a condition. "I'll marry you," she told him, "but I'm not moving in."[3] Deal! They tied the knot in July 2020.

Helen and John became part of what seems to be a growing trend among older couples in the United States: *living apart together*, or LAT. I say "seems to be" because to date, there isn't a lot of data on the topic. There is, however, anecdotal knowledge that when two older people get together, they each bring with them a full life already lived—previous romantic relationships, perhaps, or grown children or financial obligations and desires. Successfully blending these two lives while simultaneously building a new one together might require a shift away from thinking that the best route to take is traditional husband-and-wife partnership and living together 24-7.

Some research suggests LAT arrangements are an alternative to getting married, or to ever moving in together. For example, two professors at the University of Missouri interviewed twenty-five adults ages sixty to eighty-eight in LAT relationships. The majority were not married to their partners. These individuals desired "intimate companionship," the professors found, but they didn't want to give up any aspects of their full lives—their freedom!—that they had spent years building. Moreover, if they'd had caregiving responsibilities or financial issues in previous relationships, they were wary of possibly repeating uncomfortable patterns.[4]

Another study, by the National Center for Family and Marriage Research at Bowling Green State University in Ohio, looked specifically at newlyweds in LAT unions. It found that for married couples of all ages, the percentage of LAT unions doubled in the past thirty-eight years: from six percent in 1980, to thirteen percent in 2018. A little over 12 percent of newlyweds ages fifty-five to sixty-four were LAT in

2018; the percentage was almost 14 percent for newlyweds sixty-five and older.[5]

Helen told me she and John spend five nights a week together at John's place in the Bronx. "I've got my own office [in his place] and most of my clothes now and my computer and everything," she said. "But I still have my own little place here." "Here" is an apartment in Manhattan, near Central Park. "It's small, but it's lovely," Helen described. "A couple of nights a week, I come into town and . . . go out with my girlfriends. I love walking the city streets. . . . I love the sights. I love the sounds. I even like the smells. John loves to read at night and eat pizza. I really don't like pizza. So we have some nights off, and everybody's happy with that."

Setting aside affordability, Helen said arrangements like hers work only if partners "really trust each other. You've got to know where the person is." But time spent apart helps to keep a relationship fresh, she believes. Moreover, freedom with a legal obligation has given her an unexpected insight. "I now understand what a lot of teenagers know, that there's something very special about being married," Helen told me. "And it's not that you can't leave; you can always leave. It's not in my time of life a social statement; I don't need that. It's a . . ." Helen paused for a moment, then continued. "Something's enormously meaningful to marriage," she admitted, and then laughed. "I've been studying it intellectually forever, but now I get it emotionally."

When Diane Rehm and her husband want to see each other, they have a bit further to travel than Manhattan to the Bronx. Lifetime Washingtonian Diane said she'll never move from the nation's capital. John lives almost a thousand miles away, in Florida. They first met more than thirty years ago, at the home of a mutual friend. Fast forward to 2016, five years after the death of John's wife. He'd written to Diane, who'd been widowed herself after a fifty-year second marriage.

As a longtime national public media figure, Diane receives a lot of fan mail. Because of the mutual-friend connection, though, "I thought out of courtesy I should respond to his letter," Diane told me on season 1 of the podcast. "So that's what I did."

Diane mentioned to John she'd be traveling to Florida as part of her book tour, but she didn't think more of it. "So I get to Orlando," she recalled. "There are fifteen hundred people in the audience. Five hundred had paid extra to come through a line to shake my hand and have me sign their book. He was one of the five hundred—walked up, introduced himself. And I said, 'Oh, how nice to see you. And thank you for your letter, and thanks for coming.'"

She continued: "He hugged me, we kissed each other and had a photograph taken, and then he walked away. And as he walked away, he turned around and looked at me, and [at the same moment] I turned around and looked at him." *Zing!*

After Diane returned to Washington, John reached out again. He said he wanted to get to know her better, and could he come to Washington to visit? "My very proper self said, 'Well, you're welcome to come. There's a hotel a few miles away [from my home],'" Diane recalled. "'And if you'd like to come and spend a couple of days, that's fine with me.' And so he did."

That visit was the beginning of their long-distance relationship of about a year before they tied the knot in 2017. The bride was eighty-one and the groom seventy-eight. On the podcast I asked Diane why she decided to get married again instead of simply enjoying their relationship without the legalities:

DIANE REHM: I began thinking about what aloneness would be like as I grew older. And so I think that there were simply many moments watching him and being with him and seeing how much he cared for me and how much he demonstrated his care for me that helped my appreciation for him turn into love.

ME: You know, I think it's certainly understandable for people to think, *Why get married?* Because then you're going to have the legal aspects of, one of you is going to [die] before the other one goes.

DIANE: Sure.

ME: And maybe neither one of you wants to take that on again.

DIANE: Sure. But I'm old-fashioned. And for the sake of my grandchildren, I decided that living together was not a good example. So for me, the idea of living together just didn't fit my personality, did not fit my upbringing, did not fit my way of life.

ME: Right. So you want to be legally married?

DIANE: Absolutely.

ME: And at the same time, you *aren't* living together.

DIANE: Well, he maintains his work as a hospice chaplain in West Palm Beach. I maintain my work here. We are each quite comfortable.

ME: You're saying the reason you wanted to get married is so that when you do spend time together, you're spending time together as husband and wife?

DIANE: Absolutely.

ME: You're not spending time together as girlfriend and boyfriend.

DIANE: Right.

ME: You had full and complete lives when you came together.

DIANE: Exactly.

ME: So there's no need to, you know, compromise on who you already are.

DIANE: Exactly.

ME: Has there ever been a moment when you thought, *Oh, I wish John were here?*

DIANE: Sure. I miss him. But I'm still absolutely happy the way things are.

In case it didn't register, Diane chose marriage not because she wanted to adopt the traditional aspects of a legal union but because she wanted to share a bed with John when they *were* together, and Diane believes only married couples should do that. Hey, nothing wrong with her line of thinking.

Through the Reston Runners I met another LAT couple who'd wound up getting married though neither had ever expected that would be the eventual outcome. Ann and Jerry met through mutual friends in 2004, about eight years after Ann had retired as superintendent of the Statue of Liberty National Monument and Ellis Island Museum. The never married, no-kids Ann was sixty-five. She had an active social life and also volunteered as a board member for arts groups and charitable foundations. Jerry, a Brooklyn native, was seventy-one. Long divorced and the father of three grown kids, he'd traveled around the globe as an executive in an international aid organization. He too was retired, and forget the stereotype of a man needing a woman to organize his social life. A talented artist and dedicated marathoner (you should see his long, lean legs!), Jerry had a tight circle of friends.

The attraction between Ann and Jerry was immediate. Jerry wasn't interested in marriage; been there, done that. But he did want a special someone, and Ann was amenable. She found Jerry funny and interesting and decidedly unboring, unlike her previous boyfriends. So they started dating and adopted a satisfying, comfortable routine. Ann spent weekdays in her small condo in Arlington, Virginia, only a few miles from D.C. Jerry lived seventeen miles west, in Reston, in a townhouse he'd decorated to his liking. Snapshots of family members and friends covered the entire surface of his refrigerator, for example. Race bibs plastered the walls of his guest bathroom, and multiple finisher medals hung from the towel bar (I couldn't help but notice at a potluck breakfast Jerry hosted after a Saturday morning group run).

On weekends, Ann drove from Arlington to Reston to live with Jerry. During the winters, they'd travel to Florida and live together in a rented house. Along with the usual dinner types of dates, they also traveled the world and took writing and dance classes here at home.

For ten years, Ann and Jerry remained a committed LAT couple. Then Jerry had a health scare around the time of a heartbreaking loss in his former nuclear family. So when they were vacationing with friends in Croatia in May 2014 and one of them innocently asked Jerry, "How come you two never married?" Jerry thought, *Good question.* Ann had been by his side through it all, happy times and sad. Jerry wanted to give her the one thing she'd never had: marriage. So he proposed, and a surprised and gleeful Ann said yes. Five months later, she donned a long white wedding dress to walk down the aisle.[6]

About four years after they tied the knot, I talked with them in Jerry's Reston home. Ann shared that they were still LAT and also still happy. "At almost eighty, and Jerry's eighty-five, we still have a very active sex life," she told me with a giggle. "We're not dead—we're just old!"

LAT wasn't necessarily Hope's ideal relationship structure. She learned the hard way that it was the *only* way she could continue seeing Bob and maintain harmony with her four kids. Hope was a schoolteacher who also led fitness classes at her local gym. After going through a difficult divorce, her friendship with Bob had developed into something more. Ten years older, Bob was a former military member. He was also a parent, a teacher, and, like Hope, an instructor at the gym.

"I'm sort of a nerd, to be honest with you," Hope told me. "And he gets that. We can talk about science, we can talk about education, we can talk about politics. Not only that—he was taking me out to nice places. I mean, he was really, you know, courting me and just making me feel like a queen. And I really appreciated that."

But Bob also could be domineering and controlling, Hope admitted, and this became a problem when he moved in with her. At the time, Hope still had three kids at home. Her oldest son and Bob clashed frequently. "He [the son] really would take up for me—like, 'Hey, she wants the air-conditioner on, and it's only two degrees lower than you want. This is her house; she's going to have it at seventy instead of sixty-eight. What's the problem?' Bob and my son definitely collided, and it got really bad."

After Bob and her son had a physical altercation and Bob refused to apologize or take any blame for it, Hope had had enough. "And so that's when Bob had to leave," she told me. She also ended their relationship, subsequently moving from Georgia to North Carolina for a fresh start. "My son said, 'If you want to go out with him, it's okay. Don't stop going out with him because of me,'" Hope recalled. "We started having a long-distance relationship. And I just was like, you know, 'This isn't really going anywhere, and I don't want to be bothered with this anymore. I think we need to go our separate ways and really work on ourselves and where we are.'"

Bob was not persuaded. He too moved to North Carolina, in an apartment about ten minutes away from Hope's. He and Hope started dating again but this time from two separate residences. They see each other five or six times a week, she told me. He often showers her with gifts and attention, and they take walks together almost daily. "Now that [we're living apart], I find that the relationship is okay," she said.

When they have a disagreement, she ignores his phone calls and texts until he's ready to have a mature conversation about their conflict.

Hope still had two teenagers at home when we talked. Bob wasn't moving in any time soon. At this point, she couldn't figure out if she loved him enough to want things to work or if being with him was better than being alone. "I asked him, 'Can we have counseling?' He said, 'Oh yes, yes,' but it never comes to fruition. So I'm in counseling about it. So that's—yeah, I don't know. This is really raw," she admitted.

"Everybody has their faults, right?" Hope continued. "In a relationship, you tend to see the faults, and you want to make sure that this is the right person for you. And he does do great things for me. I mean, he researched how to make love to me. So, you know, he knows how to please me. I love the way he makes me feel. I love the support he gives me. I want that in a relationship. I just don't want the other stuff that's coming along with it—the nefarious ugliness that's trailing behind him. I want the stability and the sweetness and the support that he brings. And if the other stuff can just disappear, it'll be so great."

I asked Hope if she could envision a future with someone who didn't get along with her children, if a "happy blended family" was something she desired long term. Hope chuckled ruefully. "Does that really exist? Is that reality? That's what I want to know, especially for an African American female."

She added, "Sometimes you really know that maybe this isn't the right person for you. But let me just be transparent: I'm in my fifties. I have four children. So who's going to want to be around me anyway?"

I told Hope it sounded to me that she was selling herself way too short.

"Yeah, a lot of people say that," she admitted, "that I don't recognize my own value, that I'm more than I think I am. Oh well. I'm working on it. It's an ongoing process. I'll be working on it 'til the day I die, I guess."

For the LAT couples I interviewed, the key to relationship success is flexibility—not flexibility in the level of commitment itself, but in how that commitment is defined. Take octogenarians Marge and Bob as an example. At one point, the "apart" part of their LAT relationship involved Marge living in a condo Bob owned and paying him rent. (I thought this was a charming detail; the millennial WAMU podcast producers, not so much.)

Marge and Bob first met back in the 1970s when they attended the same church in Reston. Marge, a social worker, had been divorced at the age of forty-five. Bob, a real estate investor, was married to his second wife after a brief first marriage. Marge was friendly with Bob and his second wife, but they lost touch after Marge moved to New England. Decades later, she decided to return to Reston full-time to live close to her grown kids and grandchildren. By the time she moved back, Bob had been widowed for about a year.

"I saw Marge at church and didn't think too much about it. I knew she was visiting with her children," Bob recalled. "And the next week, she was there again. I said, 'Marge, when are you going back to New Hampshire?' She said, 'I'm not going back. I'm here to stay.' I thought *oh, about that.*" Bob quickly asked Marge if she'd like to have lunch with him the following Tuesday.

The strong and independent Marge told me she'd been "delighted" with Bob's invitation. Not that she needed a romantic partner, but she hadn't had much luck dating in the decades following her divorce. She remembered Bob fondly from their younger years, and she found him attractive. That lunch date quickly led to romance and travel, including a Baltic cruise.

Marge enjoyed Bob's company, but she didn't want to get married. She hadn't been anyone's wife for a very long time. "Early on, she said, 'You know, Bob, I'm a very independent person,'" Bob told me. "And I said, 'That's not a problem with me.' I expect somebody to be independent."

He continued, "We talked about the possibility of living together fairly early on in our relationship. Marge was not ready for that, first of all. And secondly, she felt that my house was too much of my late wife, which it was. And I told [Marge] the house was not that important to me, and so I decided to sell it."

Bob bought a condo within walking distance of the one Marge was renting, and they continued to date. "We had dinner [together] every night," Bob recalled, "some nights at Marge's place and the others at my place. We did that for a couple of years."

Still, Marge resisted a more traditional union. In fact, she started house hunting. She'd always wanted to buy a place of her own. She found a condo she loved, but her financial planner advised against making any purchase at her age. Marge was ready to give up on it, but then Bob had an idea. He'd buy the condo, and Marge could rent from him. "I figured Marge was the right person for me, and I was the right person for her," Bob said. "And if this is the way she wanted to live, it was okay with me." Added Marge, "I was happy with this proposal, because there were no strings attached." Bob bought the condo; Marge moved in and wrote Bob a rent check every month, always on time.

Then, in 2019, Bob had minor scheduled heart surgery. Everything went fine, he told me, but it got him thinking about life, and love. When he returned home from the hospital and Marge brought over a bottle of champagne to celebrate his good health, Bob started feeling impulsive. "I thought, *Well, I wonder if I ask her to marry me, what is she going to say? Am I going to ruin the perfectly good relationship that we have?* But then I said [to myself], *Oh, what the hell.*"

Bob didn't know it, but Marge too had been thinking about marriage. "I didn't need the formal ceremony; I was happy with just a commitment relationship," she told me. "But the more I thought about it, and the more he felt strongly about it, I thought to myself, *Well, why not? If you're going to be committed, why don't you be committed to the whole thing?*"

So when Bob blurted out a proposal, Marge said yes. If she seemed taken aback, she told me with a giggle, it was because she hadn't quite heard Bob and so was unsure exactly what he was asking her.

In April 2019, Bob and Marge gathered their families at the church where they'd first met and said "I do." The following Sunday, they brought a cake to share with the congregation. They considered maintaining their separate abodes postmarriage but ultimately decided that instead of living apart together they'd live together *together*. Bob bought yet another condo and oversaw the renovations. Marge told me that so far, the most difficult adjustment of sharing a home has been downsizing dinnerware and other household items to ensure they and their most valued possessions could comfortably fit under one roof. "We had duplicates of everything!" she recalled.

Bob and Marge may have a traditional marital living arrangement, but Marge has maintained some modern independence. She agreed with Bob's attorney that crafting a prenup would be a good idea, and she has faithfully split living expenses with her husband. "She insists on paying her share," Bob said. "She pays me the same amount every month, and it's a little bit more than what she paid me in rent at the other place. So I told her, 'It's more than you need to pay.' But she insists," Bob said, chuckling. "So I let her insist."

I have to say, I really liked this couple's story. (What *is* your problem with Marge renting from Bob, millennial podcast producers?) First, it gave me hope that the right romantic partner is somewhere out there. Basically, Marge had been alone for forty years! It also showed me what's possible when two people want to make their relationship work. As anyone who's ever been in an unsatisfying union knows, it's a slippery slope from compromising to unrequited sacrificing. Bob and Marge had a gentle give and take, and ultimately they both got what they wanted.

Hi Laura!

My partner, Rodger, and I live 10 minutes apart. My place is light and airy, while his taste is more masculine and cozy. We refer to my spot as the Summer Palace and his as the Winter Palace. Rodger had a career as a chef, so I feel indulged when I spend time at his place and he creates delectable meals. When he visits me, it's fun to nurture him with attention. With the coronavirus pandemic, Rodger and I have not sheltered at home together. Instead, we've kept up a steady phone, text, and email connection. When we feel confident that neither of us has been exposed to the virus, we'll return to our back-and-forthness.

In my younger years, I would have been itching to get married, waiting for a proposal. Or I would have been eager to move in together. Instead I find myself content with the deep bond we have forged. —S. C., California

Hi Laura,

The man who broke up with me—a blessing now that I've come through the ordeal—believed that at our age, people don't change. I couldn't disagree more. I've found midlife to be an especially ripe time for reflection and change. But I dated for many years insisting that it wasn't me who needed to change. And maybe that's the difficulty in sustaining a second-half-of-life relationship: we haven't really confronted our attachment styles and the baggage we've carried from our childhoods. One could argue that we simply need to find someone whose crazy plays well with our crazy, but I'd rather work on being less crazy. —K. J.

I am divorced after discovering my husband of 20 years was having an affair with a friend I invited to Thanksgiving dinner. Reconciliation (the usual topic that goes with fidelity) was not even part of the equation. My ex started his relationship while we were still living together in our family home and running a farm together. Now I see that divorce was the best thing to ever happen to me. I lost thirty pounds, got a pretty good marital settlement, and am closer than ever with my daughter (we both went through therapy). It took me a while to realize that I was worried about finding a partner who would bring another circumstance of abandonment to endure. Yet being vulnerable to the possibility of love is our reckoning as humans. Rarely are we wired to accept any other choice but to love and be loved again at our own peril. —A. S. F.

Hi, Laura.
I'm 68, married to a fabulous man for twelve, lived together for 30 before that. I have often pondered that if he were to predecease me, how hard would I try to become part of a couple again? So far, the answer is "not very," mostly because I don't think I could meet anyone as cool as he is, and also partly because living with someone is hard at times, and I'm not sure I could do it again. Who knows what the future brings? We make plans, and God laughs. —G. W.

Dear Laura,
I am not a gray dater yet, at 34 years of age, but I do love the stories about mature love and mature lives. I enjoy the attention on men, women, racial and sexual diversity, and so much in between. I think you tell stories with such a genuine curiosity and capture people's complex and relatable emotions for everyone to grasp. When [biological anthropologist Helen Fisher] said that [her now-husband] needed to know that he could leave her and she wouldn't crumble, gosh that was powerful. I

try to give myself the dignity and others to walk away and return in their own time and space, and I cannot stress enough how much this experience is shaping my outlook on life at the moment.

When you first released your show, I listened to several episodes with my partner who I met in early 2020. I am German, and I had a fellowship at a museum in Washington, D.C. We really bonded over the experience of listening to your stories. Unfortunately, as the year came to an end, my visa expired, and so did our relationship. We broke up with lots of heartache on my side. I have listened to all of [season 1's] episodes again, and then listened to [season 2]. Through all of this, I hear stories of people finding love later in life, I learn about how life can be mysterious sometimes and the power of giving space and evolving in your and someone else's time, and it's been a gift to discover that. I think I am taking with me the possibility of [imagining] that life and love can appear and exist in ways that I cannot control. This way I don't feel doomed [to] loneliness, and I am less scared of aging.

Your podcast has been so very meaningful to me, because our Western culture is not at all in tune with the beauty of the whole life circle. Hearing that men and women experience sexual fulfillment in their 60s more than in any other time of their life left my mouth hanging open. Can we all just take it a bit slower and allow for the best yet to come [rather than] make everything fit into our 20s and 30s? Wouldn't that make so many people less anxious about missed opportunities or hanging onto love that is not fulfilling? —Josefine W.

~

Epilogue

In May 2021, multibillionaires Bill and Melinda Gates revealed they were ending their twenty-seven-year marriage. Their surprise announcement alarmed some social conservatives and renewed media attention on gray divorce. Meanwhile, those of us who've been there, done that, understood that a longtime union breaking apart isn't necessarily a devastating outcome for either society or the parties involved. We also knew that every day, lesser-profile couples were making the difficult decision to part.

A little over a month after the Gates announcement, my friend Juan revealed via Facebook that after decades of living in Washington, D.C., he was moving into a condo on the Virginia side of the Potomac River. Left unwritten was that his wife of about thirty years wouldn't be joining him. Then, shortly before I was scheduled to see my college roommates at our annual get-together, Abby called. She didn't want to be the focus of conversation for the weekend, she said, so she was letting us all know in advance that after years of struggling, she'd finally decided to end her thirty-six-year marriage. Abby was sad, maybe even a little scared, but she also was confident she'd done everything she could to make things work. She was resolute about going forward in life on her own.

As relationships fray, new ones form. My friend Liz was married for about thirty years when her husband decided he no longer wanted to fulfill that role. After a couple of years of counseling while living stressfully in separate bedrooms under the same roof, they finally worked out the details of a property-settlement agreement. The ink was barely dry when Liz moved into a rental during the coronavirus lockdown. Socially distanced and serendipitously, she met one of her neighbors, a divorced surgeon who worked in town a few days each week. They fanned a spark into a flame, and their romantic relationship has progressed comfortably and steadily.

My Reston Runners friend Kurt and his longtime girlfriend called it quits after more than twelve years together. Turned out that basically living separate lives, albeit under the same roof, unraveled their romantic knot. Entrepreneurial Kurt's no longer in Reston; he moved to Texas for a full-time gig with benefits. He hasn't been overly thrilled about his new hometown, but his personal life picked back up after he went online and fairly quickly met a woman in the health and wellness field. Now they're living together and talking about permanently relocating out of state. (Ah, Kurt. Another good one taken.)

Kurt and I don't talk as much as we used to, but a recent text conversation made me remember not only how much fun we used to have but also how easy it is to misconstrue texts.

KURT: I'm stuck in F-ing Dallas.

ME: Ask your lady if she wants to split the Big D.

KURT: Did you ask what I think you did?

ME: ? I'm transparent. What did you think I asked?

KURT: Think you might have asked if [lady] would share me.

ME: I'm laughing so hard I'm snorting. "Split the Big D" means leaving Dallas, not sharing Kurt.

KURT: LOL. I didn't understand the message.

ME: Clearly. Although now I'm mighty curious about your self-assessment.

⌒∞⌒

Remember Jamie, who was living with her ex-mother-in-law and dating the still-married Guy? Jamie's outlaw moved out, as you learned in chapter 5, and there's even more progress to report: Guy's separation is no longer a mere aspiration. Jamie told me that Guy finally cleared his belongings out of the family home and into a place of his own. Guy and Jamie are still going strong but, unfortunately, Guy's divorce could take a while. He and his estranged wife have been fighting over the terms of the PSA, including whether to keep the big family home or sell it. Sounds to me like there's a lot of heartache and frustration all the way around, not to mention too much money being spent on attorney fees.

You read about the Professor and his long-distance, on-steroids relationship in chapter 8. Alas, it didn't work out. They broke up even before the pandemic hit. The Professor was reluctant to share details with me. On the brighter side, he's been thriving in his second career as an independent filmmaker. Also from chapter 8: twice-widowed Mark and the never-married Evamarie did not turn out to be a romantic love match, but they proved that some men and women can, indeed, be just friends.

I recommend listening to season 2's "Love After Loss" episode to hear them tell their own sweet story. As Evamarie said, getting to know Mark helped her "learn something, not just about dating but about relating to people. I've inherited my father's gift of impatience and would tend to think, *Oh, I'm not compatible with this person,* or something like that, right away. But because [Mark and I] have been talking so much, I've learned the beauty of taking your time to get to know somebody."

Added Mark, "I've really come to appreciate our relationship. We're comfortable enough talking about some personal things," including medical issues. "We've gotten to the point now where I don't think we're worried about offending each other. So this has been a very, very good relationship to have during coronaworld."

Speaking of "just friends," a couples therapist whom I also saw on my own for a few sessions told me he doubted my ex-husband and Mona would wind up romantically paired for the long term. Instead, he believed, Mona was like a transitional object Lex was using for emotional strength while extricating himself from our marriage. So whatever they were back then, I can report that today Lex and Mona really *are* just friends. At least, I think they're still in touch, as friends would be, but I don't know for sure. Because even though Lex and *I* are now just friends—well, friendly-ish—he doesn't talk to me about Mona.

He has, however, shared some details about his other romantic entanglements in the years since our split. He seems happy in his latest relationship, and I strive to be happy for him. I do worry about the impact on our kids. Linc and Sunny lovingly remind me that they're adults and that this type of concern is not in my Mom Job Description and also, probably none of my actual business. Still, you know what they say about old habits.

As for my gray-dating journey? To borrow from one of my favorite songs, *Some days are diamonds, some days are stones*. (John Denver didn't write it but he made it a hit in the early '80s. Amos Lee did it justice with his 2013 cover.) I have grown to feel happy and whole on my own and grateful that Lex gave me divorce wings. Otherwise, I would have soldiered on in that marriage forever. We had some magical moments plus two great kids together, but we really are so different that as the years ticked by, compromising steadily felt more like sacrificing. And, no surprise, we didn't exactly agree on which one of us was doing most of the compromising/sacrificing.

I highly recommend a solo stint for anyone who's sticking it out in an unhappy union because of habit, perceived societal or family pressure, financial worries, or lack of self-confidence. Sink or swim, baby. Do or die. Go for broke. (Er, maybe change that to "Get the equitable settlement to which you're entitled.") Let "better than being alone" be your ceiling—being with this person is *even better* than being alone! —and not your floor.

Still, I haven't given up on moving from Singles World back to Married Land, or to having an exclusive commitment but maybe not the legalities of marriage. So I've sought love during these later years, as you read on the previous pages. I haven't found a long-term romantic partner yet, though here's where I reveal I came close. A mutual friend introduced us; the chemistry was instant. I felt like a teenager again— all the gray-dating clichés.

Ultimately, this love wasn't mine to keep. Boy, did *that* hurt! I was sad, too. I cried and cried and cried. I had some moments of denial and self-doubt. But I didn't feel anxious or desperate or reckless or defeated, or any of the myriad destructive emotions I felt being in an unhappy marriage. Afterward, when I learned my sweet Jade probably won't live to see her eighth birthday in a month as cancer steadily grows, I didn't rage or scream. I'm chalking all of this up to progress.

I've fallen down, and I've gotten back up. Today I'm standing on strong legs, happily and hopefully continuing life's journey.

~

Acknowledgments

Writing about seeking and finding romantic love in life's later years wouldn't have been possible without the open-heartedness of men and women willing to share their true stories, comments, and questions. I'm humbled and honored to be the communications channel. Gratitude also goes to those who emailed, called, or otherwise connected me to potential stories, and everyone who has faithfully supported this project—and public radio!—despite not necessarily being gray, or a dater, especially Rebekah Gleaves Sanderlin, the Toser team, and the Reston Runners crew including Amy, Catherine, Cheryl, Kathy, Molly, and Susan.

Thanks to Claire Gerus, who always knew when Mercury was in retrograde, and the Rowman-Littlefield team, especially Suzanne Staszak-Silva and Elaine McGarraugh. Steve H., I so appreciate the middle school memory jogs.

Beautiful Geniuses Daisy Rosario and Poncie Rutsch changed the course of my professional career when they selected *Dating While Gray* for WAMU's the Pod Shop; thank you so much. Thanks also to Beautiful Geniuses and "civilian" Pod Shoppers Nichelle Calhoun, Jordan Chacon, Victoria Chamberlin, and Roger Vann for great creative energy and a whole lot of fun, and for the WAMU team who launched *Dating While Gray* into the podcast sphere, including Patrick Fort,

Jonquilyn Hill, Julia Karron, Andi McDaniel, Stephanie Shweiki, Ruth Tam, and J. J. Yore. Lawyer Bob got the ball rolling, Lawyer Matt kept it in play. Thank you, both.

Though one never forgets their first love, I'm thrilled to have forged a new relationship with WUNC, North Carolina Public Radio. It wouldn't have been possible without the enthusiastic support of content director Lindsay Foster Thomas; thank you so much. Thanks also to the entire WUNC team, especially Jenni Lawson, Charlie Shelton-Ormond, and Kamaya Truitt, for Season 2; and Katy Barron and Anisa Khalifa, who joined the fun for Season 3.

Transitioning from Married Land to Singles World was rough at times. To my actual sisters Jeanie, Lisa, Peggy, and Paula (and sister-in-law Diane), as well as my sisters from other misters: Beth, Maureen, Shevaun, and Stacy, from Supper Club; Claudia, Debbie, Denise, and Michele, the reliable Chantilly Mom Happy Hour crew; and Anne, Sue, and Weezie, my three lovely blonde roomies. Gratitude, also, to my brother Joe along with the great men in the lives of all of these women. Thank you, everyone, for the strong shoulders, wise words, and laughter. So much laughter.

Mr. T, I pity the fool who just gives up.

Julie, I'm thrilled you've joined our family.

Linc and Sunny, roots and wings—and endless, boundless, forever love. As my nana always said, *restiamo uniti*. Stick together.

Notes

Chapter One

1. Jack Gilbert, "Failing and Flying," in *Refusing Heaven: Poems* (New York: Alfred A. Knopf, 2005), 18, text available at https://www.poetryfoundation.org/poems/48132/failing-and-flying.

2. Bob Marley and the Wailers, "Three Little Birds," track 4 on *Exodus* (Island Records, 1977), vinyl album.

Chapter Two

1. Kristina S. Alcorn, *In His Own Words: Stories from the Extraordinary Life of Reston's Founder, Robert E. Simon, Jr.* (Virginia: Great Owl Books, 2016), 65.

2. Alcorn, *In His Own Words*, 83.

3. Robert D. McFadden, "Robert E. Simon Jr., Who Created a Town, Reston, Va., Dies at 101," *New York Times*, September 21, 2015, https://www.nytimes.com/2015/09/22/realestate/communities/robert-e-simon-jr-founder-of-reston-va-dies-at-101.html.

4. Gulf Reston, Inc., *A Brief History of Reston, Virginia* (Reston, VA: Gulf Reston, Inc., 1970), 17.

5. *The Reston Letter*, Dedication Issue, 4, no. 1, May 21, 1966, 1–3, archived at http://mars.gmu.edu/bitstream/handle/1920/2559/rm4_10_01 .pdf?sequence=1&isAllowed=y.

6. Gulf Reston, Inc., *Brief History of Reston*, 18.

7. "Reston, VA: New Design for an Ideal City," *Ebony*, December 1966, 91–92, archived at https://books.google.com/books?id=_5q3AoSbTGAC&q =reston#v=onepage&q&f=false.

8. Anne Chamberlin, "What Happened to Dream Town?" *Saturday Evening Post*, June 1, 1968, 64.

9. Kimberly A. Castro, "America's Best Healthy Places to Retire," *U.S. News & World Report*, September 18, 2008, 50–51, https://money.usnews.com /money/personal-finance/best-places-to-retire/articles/2008/09/18/americas -best-healthy-places-to-retire.

10. Prachi Bhardwaj, "Never Go Back to the Office: The 10 Best Places to Live if You Work from Home," *Money.com*, January 20, 2021, https://money .com/best-place-to-work-from-home/.

11. Alcorn, *In His Own Words*, 117.

12. As recounted in Rebekah Wingert-Jabi, dir., *Another Way of Living: The Story of Reston, VA*, with Vicki Wingert and Susan Jones (Reston, Virginia: Storycatcher Productions, 2015).

13. Richard Preston, *The Hot Zone: A Terrifying True Story of the Origins of the Ebola Virus* (New York: Anchor Books, 1995), 109–29, 251–61.

14. See, for example, Rescue Reston's "Updates" page, at https://www.rescue reston.org/news-updates/.

15. Norman Lear, *Even This I Get to Experience* (New York: The Penguin Press, 2014), 327.

Chapter Three

1. U.S. Census Bureau, "Table A1. Marital Status of People 15 Years and Over, by Age, Sex, and Personal Earnings: 2019," in "America's Families and Living Arrangements; 2019," Census.gov, Department of Commerce, last revised October 8, 2021, downloadable from https://www.census.gov/data /tables/2016/demo/families/cps-2019.html.

2. Diane Rehm, *Finding My Voice* (Herndon, VA: Capitol Books, 2002), 65, 73.

3. Diane Rehm, *On My Own* (New York: Alfred A. Knopf, 2016), 3–11.

4. Roxanne Roberts, "At 81, Diane Rehm Is Once Again a Blushing Bride," *Washington Post*, October 15, 2017, https://www.washingtonpost.com/lifestyle

/style/at-81-diane-rehm-is-once-again-a-blushing-bride/2017/10/15/ea5861e2
-b1c9-11e7-a908-a3470754bbb9_story.html.
5. Avery J. C. Kleinman and Kathryn Fink, prods., "Love in the Time of Retirement," *1A*, February 14, 2019, https://the1a.org/segments/2019-02-14-love
-in-the-time-of-retirement/.
6. Kleinman and Fink, "Love in the Time of Retirement."
7. New York: St. Martin's Press, 2006.
8. Bella DePaulo, "What No One Ever Told You about People Who Are
Single," filmed March 25, 2017, University of Hasselt, Diepenbeek, Limburg
(nl), Belgium, TEDxUHasselt video, 18:00 min., ,https://www.youtube.com
/watch?v=lyZysfafOAs.
9. Allison Cacich, "The Dolly in 'Rudolph' Is Actually on the Island
of Misfit Toys for a Heartbreaking Reason," *Distractify*, December 3, 2019,
https://www.distractify.com/p/why-is-the-doll-a-misfit-toy-rudolph.

Chapter Four

1. Jill R. Shah, "Struck Is a New Dating App Based on Zodiac Signs:
Skeptics Are Welcome," *Los Angeles Times*, September 7, 2020, https://www
.latimes.com/lifestyle/story/2020-09-07/struck-astrology-based-dating-app.
2. Sarah Knapton, "Loneliness Is Deadlier than Obesity, Study Suggests,"
The Telegraph, August 6, 2017, https://www.telegraph.co.uk/science/2017/08/06
/loneliness-deadlier-obesity-study-suggests/.
3. Judith Graham, "'Elder Orphans,' Without Kids or Spouses, Face Old
Age Alone," Health and Science, *Washington Post*, October 13, 2018, https://
www.washingtonpost.com/national/health-science/elder-orphans-without
-kids-or-spouses-face-old-age-alone/2018/10/12/a2c9384a-cb24-11e8a3e6
-44daa3d35ede_story.html.
4. SAGE, "LGBTQ+ Older Adults Fear Discrimination in Long-Term
Care, Need Protections: Study," SageUSA.org, August 16, 2021, https://www
.sageusa.org/news-posts/lgbtq-older-adults-fear-discrimination-in-long-term
-care-need-protections-study/.
5. Anna Fifield, "Cleaning Up After the Dead: As Family Dynamics
Change in Japan, More People Are Living by Themselves—and Dying
Alone," *Washington Post*, January 24, 2018, https://www.washingtonpost.com
/news/world/wp/2018/01/24/feature/so-many-japanese-people-die-alone
-theres-a-whole-industry-devoted-to-cleaning-up-after-them/.
6. Sheridan Prasso, "China's Divorce Spike Is a Warning to Rest of Locked-
Down World," *Bloomberg Businessweek*, March 31, 2020, https://www.bloom

berg.com/news/articles/2020-03-31/divorces-spike-in-china-after-coronavirus -quarantines.

7. Nikhil Rampal, "Many More People Commit Suicide Due to Bad Marriage than Divorce, NCRB Data Shows," *ThePrint*, November 15, 2021, https://theprint.in/india/many-more-people-commit-suicide-due-to-bad-mar riage-than-divorce-ncrb-data-shows/765923/.

8. Nicholas Bakalar, "Marriage May Bolster Recovery from Surgery," Well (blog), *New York Times*, November 2, 2015, https://well.blogs.nytimes .com/2015/11/02/marriage-may-bolster-recovery-from-surgery/.

9. Karen Kaplan, "Your Spouse May Drive You Crazy, But Your Marriage May Keep You from Losing Your Mind," *Washington Post*, December 2, 2017, https://www.washingtonpost.com/national health-science/marriage-has-its -stresses-but-it-may-lower-risk-of-dementia/2017/12/01/505d4fda-d550-11e7 -b62d-d9345cede896d_story.html.

10. U.S. Census Bureau, "Table A1. Marital Status of People," 2019.

11. Kwak Chang-yeol, "More Older Koreans Tie the Knot," *(Seoul) Chosun Ilbo*, July 14, 2020, http://english.chosun.com/site/data/html_dir/2020/07/14 /2020071401948.html.

12. *Kyodo News*, "Japan Sees Growing Number of Marriages for People Aged around 50," as published in Lifestyle, *The Jakarta Post*, June 5, 2017, https://www.thejakartapost.com/life/2017/06/05/japan-sees-growing-number -of-marriages-for-people-aged-around-50.html.

13. Julia Mio Inuma, "Japan Says Married Couples Must Have the Same Name. Now the Rule Is Up for Debate," *Washington Post*, March 12, 2021, https://www.washingtonpost.com/world/asia_pacific/japan-names-marriage -women/2021/03/11/0fd38bca-7c30-11eb-8c5e-32e47b42b51b_story.html. (Additionally, Mio Inuma responded to my email seeking clarification about the age distinction.)

14. Rachel Treisman, "In Landmark Ruling, Court Says Japan's Ban on Same-Sex Marriage Is Unconstitutional," NPR.org, March 17, 2021, https:// www.npr.org/2021/03/17/978148301/in-landmark-ruling-court-says-japans -ban-on-same-sex-marriage-is-unconstitutiona.

15. Sarah Everts, "The Truth about Pheromones," *Smithsonian Maga- zine*, March 2012, https://www.smithsonianmag.com/science-nature/the-truth -about-pheromones-100363955/.

16. Lisa Bonos, "Does My Sweaty T-shirt Turn You On? At a Pheromone Party, Singles Try to Match Using Only Their Noses," *Washington Post*, August 2, 2018, https://www.washingtonpost.com/news/soloish/wp/2018/08/02/does -my-sweaty-t-shirt-turn-you-on-at-a-pheromone-party-singles-try-to-match -using-only-their-noses/.

Chapter Six

1. Monica Anderson, Emily A. Vogels, and Erica Turner, "The Virtues and Downsides of Online Dating," Pew Research Center, February 6, 2020, https://www.pewresearch.org/internet/2020/02/06/the-virtues-and-downsides -of-online-dating/.

2. Nancy Jo Sales, *Nothing Personal: My Secret Life in the Dating App Inferno* (New York: Hachette Books, 2021), 210–11, 243, 292–94.

3. Margot Sanger-Katz, Claire Cain Miller, and Quoctrung Bui, "When 511 Epidemiologists Expect to Fly, Hug and Do 18 Other Everyday Activities Again," The Upshot, *New York Times*, June 8, 2020, https://www.nytimes.com /interactive/2020/06/08/upshot/when-epidemiologists-will-do-everyday -things-coronavirus.html.

4. John Elflein, "Share of Older U.S. Adults Fully Vaccinated against COVID-19 Nov. 2021, by State," Statista.com, November 16, 2021, https:// www.statista.com/statistics/1254292/share-of-older-us-adults-fully-vaccinated -against-covid-by-state/ (information at URL regularly updated).

5. Rich Mendez, "White House Partners with Popular Dating Apps like Tinder and Bumble to Raise Vaccine Awareness," Health and Science, CNBC.com, May 21, 2021, https://www.cnbc.com/2021/05/21/white-house -partners-with-dating-apps-to-raise-vaccine-awareness.html.

6. Suzannah Weiss, "Slow Dating: What You Need to Know," The Beehive, Bumble.com, 2021, https://thebeehive.bumble.com/datingguide-slow -dating.

7. Stephanie Mlot, "Match's New Video Chat Feature Helps Users Find Love in the Time of COVID-19," PCMag.com, April 16, 2020, https://www .pcmag.com/news/matchs-new-video-chat-feature-helps-users-find-love-in -the-time-of-covid.

8. Urvi Jacob, "Lockdown Love: Meet Zach Schleien of 'Filter Off' which Is Helping Individuals Find Their Ideal Match," Yourstory.com, April 29, 2020, https://yourstory.com/weekender/video-dating-app-filter-off-corona virus-quarantine/amp.

9. Anderson, Vogels, and Turner, "Virtues and Downsides."

10. Published in *Sociological Science* 4, no. 20 (September 18, 2017): 490–510, https://sociologicalscience.com/download/vol-4/september/SocSci _v4_490to510.pdf.

11. Lori Kogan and Shelly Volsche, "Not the Cat's Meow? The Impact of Posing with Cats on Female Perceptions of Male Dateability," *Animals* 10, no. 6 (June 9, 2020): 1007, https://www.mdpi.com/2076-2615/10/6/1007.

12. "Date Coaching Services," Smart Dating Academy, accessed January 21, 2022, https://www.smartdatingacademy.com/date-coaching.

13. Author's notes from Bela Gandhi's January 31, 2017, webinar, "Dating After 50"; recent registration information accessed at https://www.smartdating academy.com/dating-after-50.

Chapter Seven

1. Karen Nikos-Rose, "Do We Know What We Want in a Romantic Partner? Probably No More than a Random Stranger Would," News, University of California, July 9, 2020, https://www.universityofcalifornia.edu/news/do-we-know -what-we-want-romantic-partner-probably-no-more-random-stranger-would.

2. Jehan Sparks, Christine Daly, Brian M. Wilkey, Daniel C. Molden, Eli J. Finkel, and Paul W. Eastwick, "Negligible Evidence that People Desire Partners Who Uniquely Fit Their Ideals," *Journal of Experimental Social Psychology* 90 (September 2020), 103968, https://static1.square space.com/static/504114b1e4b0b97fe5a520af/t/5f03601ada29481aa880 07b2/1594056736117/Sparks2020JESP.pdf.

3. Nikos-Rose, "Do We Know What We Want."

4. "Women Who Adam Duritz Has Dated," Celebrity Hookups, Ranker. com, updated September 23, 2021, https://www.ranker.com/list/women-who -adam-duritz-has-dated/celebrityhookups.

Chapter Eight

1. Shir Filler, "Does Online Dating Mean the End of 'Meet Cute' Stories?" *Adirondack Daily Enterprise*, August 3, 2020, https://www.adirondackdaily enterprise.com/news/local-news/2020/08/does-online-dating-mean-the-end -of-meet-cute-stories/.

2. Leslie Morgan, *The Naked Truth: A Memoir; A Divorced Mom, Five New Lovers, One Audacious Adventure* (New York: Simon & Schuster, 2019), 251.

Chapter Nine

1. Nancy Kalish, *Lost and Found Lovers: Facts and Fantasies of Rekindled Romances* (New York: William Morrow, 1997), 20.

2. Nancy Kalish interviewed by Scott Simon in "Childhood Sweethearts: Unite!" *Weekend Edition Saturday*, NPR.org, May 24, 2003, https://www.npr .org/programs/weekend-edition-saturday/2003/05/24/13038566/.

3. Kalish in Simon, "Childhood Sweethearts."

4. Nancy Kalish, "Seniors Who Reunite with Old Flames," Sticky Bonds, *Psychology Today*, August 9, 2009, https://www.lostlovers.com/seniors-who-reunite-with-old-flames/.

5. Kalish, "Seniors Who Reunite."

6. John Kelly, "They Dated in High School, Broke Up, Lost Touch: A Valentine's Day Love Story," Local, *Washington Post*, February 13, 2019, https://www.washingtonpost.com/local/they-dated-in-high-school-broke-up-lost-touch-a-valentines-day-love-story/2019/02/13/6e871c36-2efd-11e9-86ab-5d02109aeb01_story.html.

7. Nancy Kalish, "Wanting to Be in the 5% Who Stay Together," Sticky Bonds, *Psychology Today*, June 1, 2014, https://www.psychologytoday.com/us/blog/sticky-bonds/201406/wanting-be-in-the-5-who-stay-together.

8. "Weddings/Celebrations; Donna Hanover, Edwin Oster," *New York Times*, August 3, 2003, https://www.nytimes.com/2003/08/03/style/weddings-celebrations-donna-hanover-edwin-oster.html.

9. Lisa Bonos, "They Met in High School. Fifty Years Later, the Pandemic Helped Them Realize They Belonged Together," Relationships, *Washington Post*, February 1, 2021, https://www.washingtonpost.com/lifestyle/2021/02/01/couple-relationship-pandemic-high-school/.

10. Bonos, "They Met in High School."

11. Tammy La Gorce, "I Do. Take 2," Vows, *New York Times*, January 3, 2020, https://www.nytimes.com/2020/01/03/fashion/weddings/Married-37-years-and-divorced-for-now-its-I-Do-Take-24.html.

12. La Gorce, "I Do."

13. Sydney Page, "A Couple Married, Then Divorced. Exactly 55 Years after Their Wedding, They Said 'I Do' Again," Inspired Life, *Washington Post*, April 20, 2020, https://www.washingtonpost.com/lifestyle/2020/04/20/couple-was-married-then-divorced-exactly-55-years-after-their-first-wedding-they-said-i-do-again/.

Chapter Ten

1. Tammy La Gorce, "When a Love Expert Falls in Love," Mini-Vows, *New York Times*, August 21, 2020, https://www.nytimes.com/2020/08/21/fashion/weddings/when-a-love-expert-falls-in-love.html.

2. La Gorce, "When a Love Expert Falls in Love."

3. La Gorce, "When a Love Expert Falls in Love."

4. Jacquelyn J. Benson and Marilyn Coleman, "Older Adults Developing a Preference for Living Apart Together," *Journal of Marriage and Family* 78, no. 3 (February 16, 2016): 797–812.

5. Krista K. Payne, Colette A. Allred, and Susan L. Brown, "FP-20-15 Married and Living Apart Together," *National Center for Family and Marriage Research Family Profiles* 229, no. 15 (2020), https://scholarworks.bgsu.edu/cgi /viewcontent.cgi?article=1228&context=ncfmr_family_profiles.

6. Megan McDonough, "On Love: Ann Belkov and Jerry Lewis," Style, *Washington Post*, January 9, 2015, https://www.washingtonpost.com/lifestyle /style/on-love-ann-belkov-and-jerry-lewis/2015/01/08/ece5df92-967a-11e4 -8005-1924ede3e54a_story.html.

Bibliography

Alcorn, Kristina S. *In His Own Words: Stories from the Extraordinary Life of Reston's Founder, Robert E. Simon Jr.* [Virginia]: Great Owl Books, 2016.

Bair, Deirdre. *Calling It Quits: Late-Life Divorce and Starting Over.* New York: Random House, 2007.

Brown, Susan L., and I-Fen Lin. "Gray Divorce: A Growing Risk Regardless of Class or Education." Council on Contemporary Families (website), October 8, 2014. https://contemporaryfamilies.org/growing-risk-brief-report/.

———. "The Gray Divorce Revolution: Rising Divorce among Middle-Aged and Older Adults, 1990–2010." *Journals of Gerontology, Series B* 67, no. 6 (November 2012): 731–41. https://academic.oup.com/psychsocgerontology/article/67/6/731/614154.

Burnham, Sophy. "Modern Love: At What Age Is Love Enthralling? 82." Modern Love. *New York Times,* February 8, 2019. https://www.nytimes.com/2019/02/08/style/modern-love-at-what-age-is-love-enthralling-82.html.

Cloud, Henry. *Necessary Endings: The Employees, Businesses, and Relationships That All of Us Have to Give Up in Order to Move Forward.* New York: HarperCollins Publishers, 2010.

Cummings, Kevin. "Love in a Time of Coronavirus: Dating Apps See Surge Despite Lockdowns." NYX Inno, March 27, 2020, https://www.bizjournals.com/dallas/inno/stories/inno-insights/2020/03/27/love-in-a-time-of-coronavirus-dating-apps-see.html (paywall).

Paulo, Bella. *Singled Out: How Singles Are Stereotyped, Stigmatized, and Ignored and Still Live Happily Ever After.* New York: St. Martin's Press, 2006.

Dreyfus, Nancy. *Talk to Me Like I'm Someone You Love: Relationship Repair in a Flash.* New York: Tarcher/Penguin, 2009.

Ellis, Abby. "After Full Lives Together, More Older Couples Are Divorcing." *New York Times,* October 30, 2015. https://www.nytimes.com/2015/10/31/your-money/after-full-lives-together-more-older-couples-are-divorcing.html.

Fisher, Helen. *The Brain in Love.* Filmed February 2008 at TED2008, Monterey, CA. Video, 15:37. https://www.ted.com/talks/helen_fisher_the_brain_in_love?language=en.

García-Hodges, Ahiza, Kalhan Rosenblatt, and Jo Ling Kent. "Dating during Coronavirus Turned Upside Down since Everything Is a Long-Distance Relationship." NBCnews.com, April 5, 2020. https://www.nbcnews.com/news/us-news/dating-during-coronavirus-turned-upside-everything-long-distance-relationship-n1175741.

Hall, Donald. "Between Solitude and Loneliness." *The New Yorker,* October 15, 2016. https://www.newyorker.com/culture/culture-desk/double-solitude.

Hanover, Donna. *My Boyfriend's Back: True Stories of Rediscovering Love with a Long-Lost Sweetheart.* New York: Hudson Street Press, 2005.

Hoffman, Leora. *Catch Me a Catch: Chronicles of a Modern-Day Matchmaker.* Port St. Lucie, FL: BookBound Media, 2020.

Jacob, Urvi. "Lockdown Love: Meet Zach Schleien of 'Filter Off' which Is Helping Individuals Find Their Ideal Match." Yourstory.com, April 29, 2020. https://yourstory.com/weekender/video-dating-app-filter-off-coronavirus-quarantine/amp.

Kalish, Nancy. *Lost and Found Lovers: Facts and Fantasies of Rekindled Romances.* New York: William Morrow, 1997.

Kirshenbaum, Mira. *I Love You but I Don't Trust You: The Complete Guide to Restoring Trust in Your Relationship.* New York: Berkley Books, 2012.

Klinenberg, Eric. *Going Solo: The Extraordinary Rise and Surprising Appeal of Living Alone.* New York: Penguin Press, 2012.

Krasnow, Iris. *The Secret Lives of Wives: Women Share What It Really Takes to Stay Married.* New York: Gotham Books, 2011.

La Gorce, Tammy. "I Do. Take 2." Vows, *New York Times,* January 3, 2020. https://www.nytimes.com/2020/01/03/fashion/weddings/Married-37-years-and-divorced-for-now-its-I-Do-Take-24.html.

———. "When a Love Expert Falls in Love." Mini-Vows, *New York Times,* August 21, 2020. https://www.nytimes.com/2020/08/21/fashion/weddings/when-a-love-expert-falls-in-love.html.

Lear, Norman. *Even This I Get to Experience.* New York: Penguin Press, 2014.

Leshnoff, Jessica. "Sexting Not Just for Kids: Plenty of Older Adults Send Racy Messages on Their Cellphones—But It's Usually a Private Matter." *AARP,* updated August 29, 2016. https://www.aarp.org/relationships/love-sex/info-11-2009/sexting_not_just_for_kids.html.

Love, Patricia, and Steven Stosny. *How to Improve Your Marriage without Talking about It.* New York: Broadway Books, 2007.

McGuirk, Leslie. *The Power of Mercury: Understanding Mercury Retrograde and Unlocking the Astrological Secrets of Communication.* New York: HarperElixir, 2016.

Milan, Anne. "Marital Status: Overview, 2011." *Statistics Canada,* last modified November 30, 2015. https://www150.statcan.gc.ca/n1/pub/91-209-x/2013001/article/11788-eng.htm.

Montenegro, Xenia P. "The Divorce Experience: A Study of Divorce at Midlife and Beyond." *AARP the Magazine,* May 2004. https://www.aarp.org/content/dam/aarp/research/surveys_statistics/general/2014/divorce.doi.10.26419%252Fres.00061.001.pdf.

Morgan, Leslie. *The Naked Truth: A Memoir; A Divorced Mom, Five New Lovers, One Audacious Adventure.* New York: Simon & Schuster, 2019.

Muzaffar, Maroosha. "Can Coronavirus Make Online Dating Safer and Global—Permanently?" Ozy.com, March 29, 2020. https://www.ozy.com/the-new-and-the-next/can-the-virus-make-online-dating-safer-and-global-permanently/291910/.

Perel, Esther. *Mating in Captivity: Reconciling the Erotic and the Domestic.* New York: HarperCollins Publishers, 2006.

Petrow, Steven. *Stupid Things I Won't Do When I Get Old: A Highly Judgmental, Unapologetically Honest Accounting of All the Things Our Elders Are Doing Wrong.* With Roseann Foley Henry. New York: Citadel Press Books, 2021.

Rehm, Diane. *On My Own.* New York: Alfred A. Knopf, 2016.

Safer, Jeanne. *I Love You, But I Hate Your Politics: How to Protect Your Intimate Relationships in a Poisonous Partisan World.* New York: All Points Books, 2019.

Sales, Nancy Jo. *Nothing Personal: My Secret Life in the Dating App Inferno.* New York: Hachette Books, 2021.

Schoen, Amy. *Get It Right This Time: How to Find and Keep Your Ideal Romantic Relationship.* Maryland: Heartmind Connection, LLC, 2007.

Schwartz, Pepper. *Prime: Adventures and Advice on Sex, Love, and the Sensual Years.* New York: HarperCollins Publishers. 2007.

Scott, Patrick. "Divorce Rates Increase for the First Time This Decade as Over-50s Untie the Knot." *Telegraph News,* October 18, 2017. https://www

.telegraph.co.uk/news/2017/10/18/divorce-rates-increase-first-time-decade
-over-50s-untie-knot/.

Spangler, Ashley, Susan L. Brown, I-Fen Linn, Anna Hammersmith, and Matthew Wright. "Divorce Timing and Economic Well-Being." FP-16-01. National Center for Family and Marriage Research, Bowling Green State University, 2016. https://www.bgsu.edu/ncfmr/resources/data/family-profiles /spangler-brown-lin-hammersmith-wright-divorce-economic-fp-16-01 .html.

Stepler, Renee. "Led by Baby Boomers, Divorce Rates Climb for America's 50+ Population." Pew Research Center, March 9, 2017. https://www.pew research.org/fact-tank/2017/03/09/led-by-baby-boomers-divorce-rates -climb-for-americas-50-population/.

Tabor, Mary. *(Re)Making Love: A Sex After Sixty Story.* North Carolina: Outer Banks Publishing Group, 2011.

Tornio, Stacy. "How to Date Later in Life if You Live in a Small Town." Firstforwomen.com, February 5, 2020. https://www.firstforwomen.com/posts /family/dating-in-small-town-over-45.

Wachtel, Ellen F. *We Love Each Other, but . . . Simple Secrets to Strengthen Your Relationship and Make Love Last.* New York: St. Martin's Griffin, 2001.

Wang, Tiffany Xingyu. "The Implications of Video Communication in the Digital Dating World." Forbes.com, March 30, 2020. https://www.forbes .com/sites/forbescommunicationscouncil/2020/03/30/the-implications-of -video-communication-in-the-digital-dating-world/?sh=4be0ae3333fe.

Wheeler, Greg. *Single Dad Essentials: The 12 Most Important Things Single Dads Need to Know.* https://gregwheelercoaching.com/book/.

Woodward Thomas, Katherine. *Conscious Uncoupling: 5 Steps to Living Happily Even After.* New York: Harmony Books, 2015.

Index

~

About the Author

Laura Stassi is creator and host of the public radio podcast *Dating While Gray*, which launched in 2020. An award-winning writer whose work has been featured in Health.mil, the *Washington Post*, and other media outlets, Laura also has authored several acclaimed nonfiction books for young readers. The mother of two grown children, Laura is a dedicated jogger along the paths and trails of Reston, Virginia, and the sandy shores of Emerald Isle, North Carolina.